The 37 Year Run

When you stop running, you start living.

Valerie Maksym

The 37 Year Run:
When you stop running, you start living.

All rights reserved. This book or any portion may not be reproduced or used in any manner without the written permission of the publisher, except for the brief quotations in a book review.

Disclaimer: The information in this book is based on my personal life experiences. What has worked for me may or may not bring the same results for everyone.

For more information about this author, visit her website at doitscaredcoaching.com

Formatting, Cover design by Blacktide International – blacktideinternational.com

Cover photo by: kblifestylephotography.com

First edition, 2025

ISBN: 979-8-993680-49-1

Copyright © 2025 Valerie Maksym

Imprint: Independently published

ACKNOWLEDGEMENTS

I want to thank my four children, who taught me that the greatest gift I could give them wasn't a perfect mother, but a healed one. Thank you for your patience as I learned to choose growth over comfort, and for showing me that breaking generational patterns is the most important work a parent can do.

To John, who proved that unconditional love isn't just possible, it's transformational. You taught me that I am enough just being me. Thank you for your unconditional love, which you give me every day.

To every woman who has ever felt like you aren't enough, or maybe you feel like you are too much, or has carried weight that wasn't yours to hold. Your story matters, and your healing matters. Your dreams are not too late to fulfill.

To my father, Thomas Jay Maksym, whose death taught me that love doesn't end, it transforms. It took me thirty-seven years to visit your grave, but it was worth the wait. This book exists because it wasn't time that healed me; it was the moment I chose to face what I'd been avoiding.

To my life coach, Angela Aja, for guiding me through the process of marketing this book.

To the friends I lost while learning to find myself, thank you for seeing who I could become, even when I couldn't see her myself. Your love wasn't wasted; it was the seed of my transformation.

To anyone who has ever sat in their car wondering how they ended up living someone else's life, this is proof that it's never too late to come home to yourself.

TABLE OF CONTENTS

INTRODUCTION   1

CHAPTER 1   5

  The Baggage That Kept Me Grounded

    Altitude Requires Letting Go

CHAPTER TWO   18

  The Vanishing Act

    How I Disappeared from My Own Life and Found My Way Back

CHAPTER THREE   29

  How I Stopped Time-Traveling to Trauma

    Triggers Aren't Warnings—They're Invitations

CHAPTER FOUR   44

  Breaking Free from the Lies You Tell Yourself

    How Limiting Beliefs Hijack Your Life and How to Fire Them

CHAPTER FIVE   54

  Walls Don't Protect, They Imprison

    Emotional Barriers Keep Love Out

CHAPTER SIX   66

  The Friendship Assassin

    How I Learned the Difference Between Performing Connection and Creating It

CHAPTER SEVEN   79

  The Thirty-Seven-Year Run

    How Avoiding One Moment of Pain Cost Me Decades of Living

CHAPTER EIGHT   **90**

    The Fierce Love That Left Scars

        How I Learned to Build Instead of Destroy the Relationships That Mattered Most

CHAPTER NINE   **109**

    The Space Between Letting Go and Finding Love

        Why Letting Go Can Feel Like Dying

CHAPTER TEN   **123**

    Serial Quitter to Dream Finisher

        Why Momentum Beats Motivation Every Single Time

CHAPTER ELEVEN   **137**

    From "All Men Cheat" to "Faithful Love Exists"

        From Speaking Limitations to Creating Possibilities

CHAPTER TWELVE   **147**

    Stop Asking Why, Start Protecting Who

        The Painting That Changed Everything

CHAPTER THIRTEEN   **159**

    How One Night Rewrote My Story

        Surviving Domestic Violence and Learning to Run Toward Life

CHAPTER FOURTEEN   **171**

    The Pilot I Finally Named

        The Day I Switched Seats with God

Valerie Maksym

INTRODUCTION

I wrote this book from the other side of the storm; from the cockpit of a life finally airborne. Three years ago, I couldn't have written these words. I was too busy white-knuckling the controls, engines screaming, burning fuel on a runway I couldn't leave. But today? Today I'm at cruising altitude, looking back at the ground I finally had the courage to leave. And I can see clearly now what kept me earthbound for so long.

This book is the flight manual I desperately searched for when I was trapped on that runway. What I needed wasn't another "how-to" guide from someone who'd never crashed. I needed a "who-did-it" story, living proof from someone who had been grounded by trauma, figured out how to release the brakes, and actually made it to the sky. I needed to know that someone else had carried everyone's baggage, had panic attacks in parking lots, lost themselves completely, and still found a way to fly. I am that proof now.

By every measure that mattered to the world, I looked successful even then. Married. Mother of four. Bodybuilder. Business owner. But I know now what those measurements hid: a woman so disconnected from herself that she was living as a stranger in her own life. At forty-four, I was having panic attacks outside grocery stores, carrying decades of other people's trauma while my own metastasized inside me. I had become an airplane at full power, going nowhere; a machine built for the sky, trapped on the ground. That woman feels like a different person now. Someone I loved, someone I honor, but someone I'll never be again.

Because I did the work. I found the broken places and healed them. I returned the emotional baggage that was never mine to carry. I faced every trigger, rewrote every pattern, reclaimed every piece of myself I'd given away. And now, from this place of victory, not perfection, but genuine transformation, I can finally give you what I couldn't find: A blueprint drawn by someone who's already flying.

Here's what makes this book different: I'm not theorizing about healing; I've done it. I'm not hoping these methods work; they rebuilt my entire life. Every framework, every tool, every practice on these pages has been tested in the fire of my own transformation. They took me from panic attacks to speaking on stages. From serial toxic relationships to authentic love with John. From people-pleasing to building a business rooted in my true voice. From hiding my faith to declaring it boldly.

Each chapter pairs up a raw story from my journey with the exact steps that got me through it. Not because I think my way is the only way, but because sometimes you need to see that someone else made it before you believe you can too.

My goal isn't to give you my answers; it's to show you how I found my answers:

How I returned the emotional baggage that was never mine to carry.

How I ran a weight check on everything in my life.

How I traded limitations for lift-off.

How I finally got airborne and stayed there.

If you're sitting in your car wondering how you became a stranger in your own life, wondering if it's too late to change, wondering if healing is possible; let me be your proof that it is. I was fifty when I finally released the brakes. Fifty-two when I took off. Fifty-four as I write these words from a life I once thought impossible.

Valerie Maksym

You're not too late. You're not too broken. You're not too anything except too ready to stay grounded any longer. Within these pages, you'll find the same frameworks I use as a coach and speaker, along with the exact practices that rebuilt my life from the inside out. But more than that, you'll find permission to stop carrying what isn't yours, to stop apologizing for wanting to fly, and to stop waiting for perfect conditions that will never come.

Your airplane is ready. The runway is clear. And I'm here, from the other side of transformation, to tell you that the view from up here is worth every terrifying moment of takeoff.

I didn't write this book because I might heal someday. I wrote it because I have healed. Because I figured out the broken places, faced them, healed them, and discovered that rock bottom was actually a runway. And now it's your turn to fly. Welcome aboard.

CHAPTER 1

The Baggage That Kept Me Grounded
Altitude Requires Letting Go

As I sat in my car on the side of the road, a clear vision came to mind. I saw my life as a symbol of an airplane, its engines thunderous and burning fuel, the harsh scent of jet fuel mingling with the humid air. The steering wheel and I became one, my pulse matching its vibration as if urging me forward, racing endlessly down a runway that never seemed to end, airborne in dreams, but grounded in practice.

That vision mirrored the weight I felt; the burdens I had unknowingly carried. In the cargo hold, chaos reigned; suitcases stacked high, each marked with a lie I believed: Too much. Not enough. Abandoned. Unworthy. Broken. The suitcase "Not Enough" brought a familiar ache to my chest, an echo of when I didn't measure up. "Abandoned" held a deep ache, a reminder of feeling forgotten. I know many of us have endured the gut-wrenching feeling like we're never enough or the fear of being left behind. These weren't just lies; they were the storm tying me to the ground.

But as I looked closer, I realized these weren't my bags at all; they belonged to other people. A teacher's words saying I wasn't smart, my mother's grief, my father's fear, a friend saying my dreams were too big, my ex's betrayal, my adult kids' personal life situations, and a friend's marriage weathering turbulence.

The 37-Year Run

Caring deeply for others, I loaded my cargo hold with their baggage, marriage stress, family drama, and financial fear until I was so weighed down my life couldn't take off. That realization changed my boundaries, not my love. I'll help you recognize the weight you're carrying. I'll show you how to unpack it. But the moment I carry your baggage; my plane can't take off either. Transformation requires that we each claim our own healing.

A voice inside said, "Valerie, you've tried to take off while carrying everyone else's baggage. This weighed your plane down and kept you grounded. You were never meant to take on others' heavy loads."

As I sat with this clarity, a question surfaced, not just for me, but for you too. Are you holding heavy baggage that isn't yours? What baggage is keeping your life from taking off? When you release excess weight, you take charge of your journey. Each bag you let go of lightens your load and propels you closer to takeoff. Picture yourself as the hero who discards what no longer serves you, feeling lighter and more capable with each release. To begin this journey today, identify one piece of baggage that's not yours to carry. Take a deep breath and set it down. This small act can spark a transformation, allowing you to reach your true potential.

The Aircraft That Never Left the Ground

The vision exposed what I'd been doing for thirty-seven years: collecting other people's trauma like it was mine to heal. I absorbed their childhood wounds, their unprocessed grief, their generational pain, carrying it all in my body until I couldn't tell where their damage ended, and I began. Two marriages collapsed under that weight. Both times, I blamed myself when they couldn't love me, never recognizing that broken people break things, including the hearts that try to save them. I believed every cruel word they spoke in their pain was the truth about who I was. So, I made myself smaller, quieter, and less ambitious. My dreams of changing lives through coaching and speaking? I locked them away, afraid that reaching for more would prove I was "too much" like they said.

The physical toll was undeniable. My nervous system stayed locked in survival mode, heart racing at grocery stores, shoulders permanently tensed, and unable to take a full, deep breath for years. At forty-four, my body was screaming truths my mind had been too afraid to hear. That's when I made the decision that changed everything: I would keep only what was truly mine. Not their pain, not their limitations, not their definitions of who I should be. Just my worth, raw, unedited, and finally uncaged. One by one, I began releasing decades of stored trauma, and with each piece I let go of, I felt my wings remember what they were made for.

The Science Behind Inherited Trauma

Reclaiming my worth required understanding exactly what I was carrying and why. So, I traced every trigger, every pattern, and every self-destructive habit back to its root. What I found changed everything: the trauma in my body wasn't all mine. Some of it had been handed down through bloodlines: grandmother to mother to daughter, like a curse no one knew how to break. Dr. Rachel Yehuda's research gave me the science behind what I intuitively knew: trauma doesn't just live in our memories; it lives in our cells, in our DNA, and we pass it to our children before they take their first breath. That knowledge nearly broke me. My kids were carrying wounds from battles they never fought, from grief that was never theirs.

The 37-Year Run

In that moment, a wave of fear washed over me. I was scared to confront the possibility that my struggles were not just mine, but a shadow cast by my ancestors. The fear of uncovering painful family histories and recognizing my role in this cycle made me pause. Yet, this vulnerability became my compass. The constant worry, the inability to relax, anxiety, and depression. They were coping mechanisms handed down from family members who'd survived their own trauma. This scientific understanding helped me make sense of my experiences, laying out the groundwork for new healing strategies. With this newfound awareness, I was not only able to confront these fears but also to see a glimpse of hope. Understanding that these struggles could be addressed and that healing was possible through conscious effort and change reassured me. It set the stage for a journey where vulnerability turned into strength, and awareness opened doors to healing.

Here's one healing practice that became a vital part of my journey. Each morning, I would wake up an hour earlier than usual to give myself time to reprogram my flight controls and thought patterns. One of my morning rituals is to repeat my daily affirmation: I am worthy of healing and growth. As I inhale, I imagine fueling my mind with all the good I desire and positivity; as I exhale, I release inherited fears, negative thoughts, and anxieties, offloading excess cargo. After repeating this affirmation, I try to notice the physical sensations in my body. My shoulders begin to relax, and I feel a steady rhythm in my breath, signaling a newfound sense of calm and safety. This small, consistent action helps recalibrate my mindset, turning programmed pain into an opportunity for transformation and smoother ascent.

Here's the game changer. Just as trauma can be inherited, so can healing. Dr. Gabor Maté's research shows that when one person in a family system chooses to heal their inherited trauma, it creates a "healing rupture" affecting the entire family line, past, present, and future. The moment I decided to stop carrying other people's pain, grief, anxiety, and fears, I didn't just free myself. I freed my children from inheriting those wounds. Watching them naturally begin to heal as I healed showed me the invisible chains I had finally broken. Now I see the bigger picture. Healing and change are possible for the entire family when one person becomes the catalyst for change.

The Baggage Audit That Changed Everything

That day on the roadside inspired a new action: inventory what was and wasn't mine to carry. Among my findings, a friend's opinion that men always leave. Her truth, not mine. My father died; he chose to leave. That's a tragedy, not abandonment. My ex's actions that spoke you're not enough to keep someone faithful. His choice, not my inadequacy. A friend's critique, You're too much, too direct, too honest. That's their discomfort with authenticity; not proof I should shrink. A childhood belief: If you're perfect, maybe they'll stay. A twelve-year-old's desperate need to control is not a life strategy. Once I separated what was mine from what was inherited or assigned, I found a simple truth: I am a woman who survived loss, betrayal, and disappointment and still believes in love and possibility. That's not baggage, that's resilience.

The Moment I Chose Flight Over Grounding

In my car, I made a decision that changed everything. I refused to be held back by others' unresolved pain. The choice was clear, either continue drowning in others' problems or release and let go of what wasn't mine. First, I stopped giving emotional energy to my adult kids' decisions and other people's dramas. Their choices, their consequences, their growth. I stepped back and let my children take ownership of their decisions while encouraging them to become the best version of themself. Letting go of others' problems freed up unexpected space. The logic was simple, time spent carrying others' baggage was time lost building my own life.

The W.E.I.G.H.T. Method: Your Baggage Audit System

After that roadside revelation, I developed what I call The W.E.I.G.H.T. Method. A systematic approach to identifying and releasing emotional baggage that isn't yours. This method is designed to free you from inherited limits in just minutes a day. It is intended for anyone, no matter where you are on your journey. Whether you're just beginning to recognize the weight you carry, or you've been on this path for a while. Follow these steps and watch your old life become unrecognizable. Starting this process can feel scary and overwhelming; it's completely normal to have those feelings. Remember that small steps are powerful, and even the slightest change can be enough to start your journey toward a lighter, more liberated life. I can still recall the first time I consciously applied the W.E.I.G.H.T. Method to my life. I was sitting at home, feeling overwhelmed by the expectations and judgments of others. All the voices in my head echoed past criticisms like a relentless chorus. I decided to write them down, and with each word I put on paper, I began to dissect where they came from. Surprisingly, I discovered that many were echoes of a friend's cautionary remarks from years ago. Recognizing this, I told myself that I would no longer carry these thoughts nor let them define my path. As I closed my journal, a sense of relief and newfound freedom washed over me. That small action became a cornerstone for my personal transformation, and it affirmed that this method could indeed work wonders.

W stands for WRITE- Write down your limiting beliefs. This step involves writing down every negative thing you believe about yourself, including those internal voices that love to list everything you can't do. Be completely honest as you write down what you think you can't do, can't have, or can't become. The goal is to see these beliefs clearly so you can begin to address them.

Examples:

"I'm too old to start over."

"I don't have what it takes to run my own business."

"I'm not the kind of person who deserves a faithful partner."

"I'm too much for people, too intense, too direct."

"I always mess things up eventually."

"I'm not smart enough to go back to school."

E is for EXAMINE -Take a closer look at the origin of each belief on your list. Whose voice are you really hearing? Is it your mother's insecurities, your father's judgment, an ex's criticism, a friend's jealousy, or a teacher's offhand remark? Naming the source helps you separate your own truth from the beliefs you've inherited.

Ask yourself how these beliefs may have once served a purpose; perhaps they helped you feel safe or cope with difficult situations. But while they may have protected you in the past, they could now be holding you back. Recognizing this shift allows you to meet yourself with compassion, and that's often where real change begins.

Examples of inherited beliefs and their sources:

"I'm too old to start over."
→ This is a woman's voice after her husband left during their golden years.

"At my age, who's going to want me?"
→ Echoes of an ex-husband's words during a divorce.

"I don't have what it takes."
→ An ex's voice again: "You'll never make it without me."

"I'm too much."
→ A friend's voice, "You're exhausting to be around."

"I always mess things up." → A parent's frustrated outburst when you were a child: "Can't you do anything right?"

I stands for IDENTIFY- Identify what belongs to you. Look at your list and circle only the beliefs that came directly from your choices or experiences, not from what others said or implied about your character. This helps you distinguish between your genuine challenges and those imposed by others.

Examples:

✓ "I chose to stay in that marriage too long" (yours)

✗ "That means I'm weak" (their interpretation)

✓ "I overreacted during our argument" (yours)

✗ "That means I'm impossible to love" (their projection)

G means GIVE- Give back what Isn't yours. For each belief that came from someone else, write a statement such as, this belief belongs to [person's name]. I return it to them and take back my power to move forward. This process intentionally releases what is not yours to carry.

Examples:

"The belief that I'm 'too much' belongs to a former college roommate.

Discomfort with my authenticity stemmed from her fear of being real, not evidence that I should shrink. I return this to her and reclaim my right to take up space."

"The fear that 'all men cheat' belongs to a close friend. Her pain from her husband's betrayal became my relationship template, but it's not my truth. I return this to her and reclaim my ability to trust wisely.

H stands for HONOR- Honor your actual story. Replace every belief you've returned with an affirmation that reflects your true self. Ground it in your own resilience, growth, and capacity for love. This reinforces your sense of identity based on your experience, not others' perceptions.

Examples: Replace: "I'm bad at relationships" With "I'm someone who loves deeply and has learned to set boundaries."

Replace: "I'm not successful" With: "I'm someone who raised my children while building a career and survived a divorce with my heart still open.

T is to TAKE FLIGHT. Make a specific, actionable decision that reflects your true worth rather than the limitations you've inherited. Examples include applying for a new job, leaving an unhealthy relationship, or pursuing a long-held dream. This step commits you to moving toward authenticity and freedom. To kickstart this process, make a 24-hour commitment. Before tomorrow night, take one action that scares you, such as signing up for that class you have been putting off, applying for that job, or making a phone call for an opportunity you've been avoiding. This immediate step will help you gain momentum and begin your journey toward your accurate flight.

Examples: Sign up for the fitness class or sports competition of your choice despite the voice saying, "You aren't strong enough, talented enough, or you don't have the right type of body." Enroll in the business course instead of listening to "you're not smart enough." Limit your time with the people who constantly criticize, rather than staying small to keep the peace. Book the

The 37-Year Run

solo trip abroad despite "what will people think?" Start dating again despite the feeling that you will never find the one.

Each step should be a specific, actionable choice that moves you from limitation to authentic power. To maintain your climb and momentum, use supportive practices to keep you airborne. Engage with friends, family, or community groups for encouragement and perspective. Supportive environments can include networking or social groups, church, or local community activities where fellow residents connect. Keep a journal to track your progress and insights. Celebrate small victories to reinforce your progress and commitment. By practicing these habits, you stay inspired and on your own path of empowerment. If releasing baggage triggers overwhelming emotions, consider reaching out to a therapist, counselor or life coach. You can also lean into your faith and pray or practice grounding techniques, such as deep breathing or meditation. Remember, seeking help is a sign of strength, not weakness.

The Takeoff That Nearly Didn't Happen

Three months after my roadside awakening, I faced my first real test of applying this new understanding. Years earlier, I competed in bodybuilding competitions. This dream had been with me since my teenage years. Even on stage, I carried inherited voices: You don't have the right body type, you aren't coordinated, and you are too shy. People will think you're ridiculous up there with stretch marks on your stomach from having four babies. You're trying too hard to prove something. I once mistook those voices for my own, believing they were a realistic self-assessment. But now I can see whose voices they really are. Like my ex's voice, you don't have a body for competing, trying to keep me small. A friend from church said, women shouldn't show off their bodies like that, expressing her own fear of judgment. Even after taking first place in one category, I couldn't truly celebrate. The weight of others' opinions and their discomfort still clung to me like chains. Now I understand that I had been competing while being weighed down by their baggage. I achieved my dream ,but couldn't fully celebrate because of the limitations I felt were put on me. For the first time, I understood the difference between achieving dreams while carrying others' fears and choosing my own courage without that extra weight.

Your Flight Plan Assessment

Take a moment to answer these questions.

What dreams have you postponed because someone told you that you couldn't, shouldn't, or weren't worthy of achieving them?

Whose voice plays in your head when you consider taking risks, changing careers, or pursuing what lights you up?

What would you attempt if you knew that the only opinion that mattered was your own?

When was the last time you made a significant decision based purely on what you wanted, not what others expected or approved of?

Your answers will reveal whose baggage you've been carrying and what dreams have been waiting for you to choose flight over familiar ground.

The Sky Is Waiting

Your airplane has been on the runway long enough. The engines are ready. The destination is set. The sky is calling your name. You can't reach your altitude carrying everyone else's weight. Remember, you are not alone. Surround yourself with a community of people who have chosen to fly and reject others' limitations. You may ask: What about the people who gave me their baggage? They'll have to figure out their journey just like you are figuring out yours. Your role isn't to carry their load; it's to show what's possible when you fly. The people who matter most need to see you soar. Your dreams need someone brave enough to choose them over others' comfort. The world needs you at full altitude, not grounded. With conviction, say out loud, "Today, I choose to fly." This is your moment. Your decision. Your new beginning. You're not the first person to make this choice, and you won't be the last. However, you might be the one who finally breaks the cycle in your family or among your friend group. Share your story today. Invite someone to walk this path with you.

As you progress on your journey, take the time to share your victories, challenges, and ongoing experiences with those around you. Don't heal in silence. When you share your progress, you create accountability for yourself and light the path for others who are still finding their way. Together, you can soar higher. Take the initiative to connect, inspire, and support everyone you meet, helping them reach their full potential. The journey grows stronger when you lead the way. To make this commitment even more powerful, I have a challenge for you today. What belief will you choose to release? And what action will you take that reflects this newfound freedom? Share your chosen beliefs and actions with someone you trust. Let your declaration inspire others to join you on this transformative journey. Together, let's convert reflection into a public commitment, and watch how the choice to fly inspires others to do the same.

The Clearance You've Been Waiting For

Today in this present moment, you have clearance for take-off. You don't have to wait until you lose ten pounds, find the perfect partner, get your finances together, or overcome all your fears. The runway is clear. The weather is perfect. Your flight plan is approved. The only question left is: will you take full responsibility for your own takeoff, or will you spend another decade as a storage facility for other people's unresolved pain? Your baggage claim ticket expires today. It's time to prioritize altitude over the comfort of others. It's time to choose flight over familiar suffering. It's time to trade baggage for wings. The sky is waiting. Your dreams are calling. You are cleared for takeoff. As you prepare for this new journey, I encourage you to start with one small step. Write down one belief that you want to release today. Let this be your initial action toward a more fulfilled life. Use it as a tangible reminder that you are choosing to fly.

CHAPTER TWO

The Vanishing Act

How I Disappeared from My Own Life and Found My Way Back

I was sitting across from the man who had just confessed to cheating on me. Instead of reacting with anger or pain, I asked, "So where should we go to dinner tonight?" My voice sounded calm, though inside I felt like I was falling apart. I suggested restaurants, scrolling through reviews, as if nothing life-changing had happened. In that moment, I realized my instinct was to hide my feelings and prioritize peace over expressing my hurt. I wasn't just lacking self-love; I didn't recognize myself at all. My need to avoid discomfort was so strong that I erased myself entirely, even as my trust was destroyed.

The Sleepless Nights That Broke Me

For the next three weeks, I didn't get much sleep. Not because I was heartbroken, though I was, but because my mind was trapped in an endless loop that I couldn't stop or solve. Every night, I'd lie in bed as my brain ran the same broken program.

Confront him about the betrayal → He might leave → I'll be alone → I can't handle being alone → Don't confront him → But he cheated → Confront him → He might leave...and the loop continued to replay.

Round and round, hour after hour it played, and my mind wanted justice, but my terror of abandonment wanted peace. The two forces pulled against each other until I felt like I was being torn in half. I'd get up at 3 AM and walk circles around my house, my nervous system so fried from the contradiction that I couldn't even sit still. By dawn, I'd be exhausted but still no closer to a solution. How do you confront someone when confrontation might cost you the only thing standing between you and the void of being alone with yourself?

How I Trained Myself to Vanish

What I didn't understand then was that I was suffering from a lack of self-concept clarity, the inability to define myself outside of others' needs and opinions. Every sleepless night, my mind felt like it was short-circuiting, programmed to prioritize everyone else's comfort over my own truth.

People with low self-concept clarity often fall into two patterns:

They depend on external validation to feel worthy.

They avoid conflict at all costs, even if it means silencing their own truth.

The heartbreaking part is that the more you erase yourself to keep others comfortable, the more your brain reinforces the belief that your needs don't matter. You literally train yourself to self-abandon. Every time I said "I don't care" when I absolutely did, I was teaching my brain that my preferences were irrelevant. Every time I laughed at jokes that hurt me, I was programming myself to prioritize others' comfort over my own truth. And every time I let silence speak where my heart wanted to scream, I was reinforcing the idea that my feelings were something to hide, rather than to honor. I was a people-pleaser, avoiding conflict to keep others happy. But while doing so, the true, authentic me vanished.

The Vacation Planning That Exposed Everything

Three days after his confession, I did something that would later horrify my friend. I started researching romantic getaways to "work things out." Not because I had forgiven him; I hadn't even begun to process what forgiveness would mean, but

The 37-Year Run

because facing the truth of what he'd done felt more terrifying than pretending it hadn't happened.

I spent hours online, reading reviews of couples' retreats, and comparing amenities at romantic resorts. I bookmarked a place in Sedona that specialized in "trust rebuilding," and another in Napa that promised "relationship renewal." I poured more energy into planning our reconciliation vacation than I had ever invested in asking myself what I truly needed from a partner.

When she called to check on me and I casually mentioned comparing hotel packages, the silence on the other end was so long I thought the call had dropped. "Valerie," she finally said, her voice stern but controlled, "he cheated on you three days ago. Why are you planning a vacation instead of planning your exit plan? The answer that came out of my mouth shocked us both. "Because I'm scared to be alone. And being with someone who betrays me feels safer than being alone with myself." Those words hung in the silence, leaving me exposed with nowhere to hide. I had just spoken the painful truth: I would rather vacation with a cheater than face going to dinner alone.

The Physical Cost of Disappearing

The sleepless night was just the beginning. My body had been keeping the score every time I erased myself, and now, the bill was coming due. My shoulders lived somewhere near my ears, permanently braced for the next emotional blow. My stomach felt like I'd swallowed broken glass, clenched tight from all the words I never said. I developed a nervous laugh that bubbled up at the worst times, like when he criticized my cooking or mocked my "dramatic" emotions. Even simple questions like *"What movie do you want to watch?"* or *"Where should we eat?"* could trigger panic attacks. My nervous system would spike into fight-or-flight because I no longer knew how to access my own beliefs.

Food had lost its taste as I sat across from him at restaurants I'd chosen to please him, mechanically chewing meals that might as well have been cardboard. My body had become so disconnected from my authentic self that even basic sensory experiences felt muted, as if I were living behind a wall of glass, watching my life instead of living it.

The Pattern I Recognized Everywhere

That night, alone in my home for the first time in months, something shifted. I realized I wasn't the only one who had learned to disappear to survive; I had seen this pattern reflected in the lives of people I cared about. My friend stayed with a man who emotionally abused her, saying, "At least he doesn't hit me." Another worked weekends for a boss who screamed at her, insisting, "Jobs are hard to find." A woman I knew apologized for crying during a hard moment, saying, "I didn't mean to make anyone uncomfortable." In that quiet moment, I saw it clearly: we had all been shrinking ourselves to stay connected, believing that silence kept us safe. I had spent years making myself smaller to avoid abandonment, hiding my needs to keep others comfortable, and convincing myself that disappearing was the price of being loved.

But the real shock wasn't just seeing the pattern; it was realizing how deeply I had internalized it. I had become so skilled at vanishing that when someone asked me a direct question, such as what I wanted to drink, I sometimes forgot how to answer. I had trained myself to be invisible, and in doing so, I had lost complete sight of who I was.

The 37-Year Run

The E.X.I.S.T Method: How to Stop Disappearing

Disappearing may feel like protection, but over time, it becomes a prison. When you keep shrinking yourself to fit others' expectations, you lose access to your own voice, your own needs, and your own life. You miss the chance to live authentically, and the world misses out on the unique gifts only you can offer. If you continue to vanish, you'll never know the deep fulfillment that comes from showing up as your true self.

The E.X.I.S.T method is about reclaiming your space, one step at a time.

E – EXAMINE Your Disappearing Patterns

Start by writing down the specific ways you tend to isolate yourself from others and opportunities. When I did this, the list was devastating. I said *"I don't care"* when asked about restaurants, movies, or weekend plans, because I didn't want to be a burden. I agreed to social events I dreaded, because I was terrified of disappointing anyone. I apologized for having needs: "Sorry, I know this is stupid, but." I adjusted my laugh, my opinions, even my posture to match whoever I was with. I asked, *"What do you want?"* instead of ever knowing what I wanted. And instead of questioning why people made cruel jokes, I searched online for *"how to be less offended or triggered by others' rude remarks."* Each of these moments was a quiet act of self-erasure. Naming them was the first step toward reclaiming my voice.

X – CROSS OUT the People-Pleasing Voice

Start by identifying the voice that says, *"Don't rock the boat,"* or *"Their happiness matters more than yours."* Whose voice is that, really? For me, it was a chorus of whispers I'd absorbed over the years. It was every teacher who rewarded my quiet compliance with gold stars. Coaches who praised players for *"not causing drama."* Friends who called me *"easy-going"* when I never actually voiced a preference. It was the subtle messaging that told me being accommodating, flexible, and agreeable made me lovable. But none of those voices were mine. They taught me that disappearing was noble, but I'm learning that being visible is necessary.

I – INVENTORY Of Your Authentic Beliefs

This was the hardest part. After years of disappearing, I had to relearn what I actually wanted. Where did I like to eat? Mexican food, always. How did I enjoy spending weekends? Poolside relaxation and deep, meaningful conversations over dinner. Bars were never my thing. What made me laugh? Clever puns and wordplay. Humor that mocked people's looks or mistakes just felt cruel. What were my deal-breakers? People who hid cruelty behind jokes, kept me at arm's length emotionally, lied, or performed instead of being authentic. And the dreams I had abandoned? Writing. Traveling solo. Launching my coaching and speaking business. Learning a second language. Dancing. I even once searched *"how to be less sensitive,"* when the real question should've been *"why do I feel like I have to toughen up to be accepted?"*

S - SPEAK One Truth Daily

Every day, voice out loud one authentic preference, even if it feels terrifying.

"Actually, I'd prefer Mexican food tonight."

"I'm not comfortable with that joke."

"I need some time to think about this."

"That doesn't work for me."

"I'm going to stay home tonight; I'm tired."

"I'm going to have to say no to your request."

The 37-Year Run

T – TRUST Your Right to Exist

This was the game changer. I wasn't asking for permission to have beliefs, needs, or preferences. I was finally acknowledging that I already had them. My wants, my boundaries, and my opinions weren't suggestions open for negotiation. They were valid expressions of who I am. They weren't too much, or not enough; they were mine. Learning to trust that truth was the beginning of reclaiming my space in the world.

The Daughter Test That Shattered My World

The breakthrough came months later during a conversation with a friend. She asked a question that completely dismantled my internal operating system. "If your daughter came to you after discovering her partner had cheated, what would you tell her?" The answer rolled off my tongue with a fierceness that surprised us both. "I'd tell her she deserves better. I'd tell her to leave immediately. I'd tell her that staying teaches him that cheating is acceptable, and that she's available for mistreatment." Without hesitation, I said, "I'd tell her that love shouldn't require her to shrink herself to fit into someone else's limitations. I'd probably shake her and ask what happened to her self-respect." My friend leaned in and asked, "So why are you giving yourself different advice than you'd give someone you love?" The question hit like a physical blow. I doubled over in my chair, finally seeing the toxic double standard I had been living by. Everyone else deserves protection, advocacy, and fierce love. But me? I accepted whatever crumbs others were willing to offer. The truth blazed through me. I had been my own worst enemy, my harshest critic, and my most neglectful caretaker.

Trusting My Right to Exist

Learning to treat myself with the kindness I'd freely give a friend or even a stranger changed everything. But what blindsided me was the physical rewiring that followed. As I practiced self-compassion, foreign as it felt, my brain began rebuilding itself from the inside out. For the first time in years, I could sit with my own pain without numbing out or running. My cortisol dropped. My shoulders relaxed. The fog lifted. I started making decisions from a place of clarity instead of desperation. Here's what I discovered: when you stop abandoning yourself, your brain stops abandoning you. But nobody warns you that self-compassion feels like death when you've never experienced it before.

For me, it literally felt like dying. When you've spent years shapeshifting into whoever others needed, finding your authentic self isn't beautiful; it's brutal. You're not just changing thoughts; you're demolishing an entire identity built on self-betrayal. Every act of kindness toward yourself feels like a betrayal to everyone you've been trained to serve. Every boundary feels like abandonment. Every "no" feels like a small death, because it is. You're killing the version of yourself that survived by disappearing, and birthing someone who insists on being seen.

The 30-Day Being Present Challenge

Here's the specific protocol that woke me up and brought me back to life.

Week 1: Notice When You Disappear - Every time you say "I don't care" or agree to something you dislike, write it down. No judgment, just awareness. You can't change what you can't see. My list from week 1 was several pages long. Pages full of ways I'd been disappearing that I'd been unconscious of.

Week 2: Voice One Preference Daily- Start small. Choose where to eat. Pick the movie. Express an opinion about the weather. Build the muscles of having wants. The first time I said, "Actually, I'd prefer the romantic comedy over the action movie," my date looked at me and said, "Your wish is my command."

Week 3: Set One Boundary Weekly- Say no to one thing that drains you. Cancel one plan you don't want. Speak up about one thing that bothers you. Notice that the world doesn't end when you have limits. The day I told my friend I didn't want to be her daily therapist anymore, I felt like jumping off a cliff. She was shocked, then became angry, and eventually understood and showed respect. Our friendship grew stronger, not weaker, once she realized that all she had been doing was dumping her problems on me.

Week 4: Make one Decision- This is based solely on what you want. That's the graduation test. Pick something, anything, driven by pure desire. Not what others expect. Not what you think you 'should' want. What you want, one hundred percent. I booked a trip to Mexico. The old me would have polled everyone, then canceled to avoid looking selfish. The new me? I bought the ticket and announced it."

The Mirror Moment That Saved My Life

About nine months after the breakup with the cheater, I started showing up for myself. I looked in my bathroom mirror and saw someone I genuinely liked spending time with. Not the anxious, apologetic woman who used to stare back at me, shoulders hunched in permanent apology. This woman stood straight. She looked me in the eye. She had regained her glow, her expressions lively and full of energy. She looked like someone whose opinion mattered, whose needs counted, whose happiness was worth fighting for. I half-expected the mirror to send me an invoice for my own personal restoration project.

Most importantly, I saw someone who would never again ask a betrayer where he wanted to go to dinner because she'd be too busy showing him where to find the door. The difference wasn't that I'd suddenly mastered self-love. The difference was that I'd finally stopped erasing myself.

Becoming Someone to Love

Two years later, I met John. But this time, everything felt different. When he asked where I wanted to go for dinner, I gave him an answer, no more defaulting to "I don't care." When he asked what I thought about something, I shared my honest opinion, instead of trying to guess what he wanted to hear. When he showed interest in me, I didn't shrink into grateful acceptance. I stayed present, curious to see if I was interested in him too. For the first time in my adult life, *I* was there, fully, wholly, and unapologetically. There was finally a "me" to be loved. The result? A marriage built not on need or incompleteness, but on two emotionally healthy, happy people choosing each other, whole on their own, stronger together.

Your Existence Assignment

When was the last time you made a decision based purely on what you wanted, without considering how it would affect everyone else's comfort? If you can't remember, you've probably been disappearing too. Your assignment for tomorrow:

Be your authentic self for one full day. Voice your preferences, honor your needs, set one boundary, and make one decision based on what you want. Not because you're selfish, but because you can't fill anyone else's cup from an empty pitcher.

Stop Disappearing. Step Into Your Life.

Your life is waiting for you to show up. This week, someone will ask you what you want for dinner, where you'd like to go, or what you think about something that matters. And in that moment, in those next ten seconds, your answer will reveal everything. Are you living your life, or performing someone else's version of it? Stop fading into the background. Start living with intention. Start today. Let this be your mantra; "I am enough; therefore, I choose." Let it guide you at every dinner table, in every decision, and in every quiet moment of self-reflection. Let it echo through your daily life as a reminder that your voice matters, your choices shape your path, and your presence is powerful.

CHAPTER THREE

How I Stopped Time-Traveling to Trauma

Triggers Aren't Warnings—They're Invitations

The coffee mug warmed my palms as steam curled between us in the morning light through my kitchen window. John sat across from me at the high-top table I bought for one, now shared with someone who made Sundays feel like a gift. Without saying a word, he settled into the sunlit chair and was scrolling through his phone with that focused concentration he got when planning his adventures. John enjoyed his own company, having traveled solo since he was a young boy living in Africa. Independence was pure joy for him. "So, I'm going to Vegas next month," he said casually, not looking up. "There's this poker tournament I signed up for months ago. It should be fun." Two words. Vegas weekend. My chest tightened; it felt like a python slowly coiling around my lungs. The coffee mug slipped from my hands. I caught it just before it crashed onto the floor. My stomach didn't just drop, it free-fell through the floor, through the ground, straight to the middle of the earth. John's voice became distant, as if he were speaking underwater. The kitchen walls seemed to pulse inward. My hands started trembling so uncontrollably that I had to press them flat against the cool wood of the table to make them stop. And then came the voice. That familiar, venomous whisper that I thought I'd silenced forever. "Here we go again. Vegas. You know what happens in Vegas. Remember the last time? Remember how you weren't enough then either? Remember finding those texts on your ex's phone? Remember how he looked you dead in the eye and called you crazy for asking questions?"

The 37-Year Run

The Time Machine in My Kitchen

In that split second, I wasn't a woman who had learned to value herself, standing in her own sunlit kitchen with a man who brought love and peace to her life every day. I reverted to my younger self, sitting in a different kitchen, in a different life, holding a different phone with text and memories that shattered my world. Here's what nobody tells you about triggers: They don't just bring back memories; they build a time machine, stuff you inside, and lock the door. You're not remembering trauma; you're living in it again, breathing the same suffocating air, feeling the same crushing weight on your chest. Standing there with John, I was experiencing a flashback. I was in 2019, feeling that same humiliation, that same not-enoughness, that same terror that love was just a temporary loan that could be revoked without warning. My brain had hijacked my present moment and was running it through the filter of someone else's betrayal. John, kind and loyal, who brought me medicine and food when I was sick and had never given me a single reason to doubt him. He was being tried in my mental courtroom for crimes he'd never committed. The old story was grabbing the steering wheel of my life, and it was heading straight for a cliff.

The Science Behind Emotional Time Travel

I didn't know then that I was experiencing what's called "trauma reenactment." My nervous system couldn't distinguish between past danger and present safety. John's mention of Vegas triggered a fight-or-flight response, even though the threat was only in my memory. Trauma lives in the body, not the logical mind. When triggered, the thinking brain shuts down, and the survival brain takes over. Logically, I knew John wasn't my ex, but my body only cared about survival.

Valerie Maksym

The Ten-Second Choice That Saved My Future

I had seconds before panic would take over, before I might push away the best man I'd met. In those seconds, I chose to fight for the present. "I need a minute," I said. John looked up, concerned flashing in his eyes, but he didn't try to fix me. "Of course," he replied. I walked to the bathroom, reminding myself; this is now. Looking in the mirror at my flushed, stressed face, I spoke softly out loud: "I see you're scared. You remember what happened before and want to protect us. But that was your ex. This is John. That was 2019. This is now. That was betrayal. This is trust."

The Conversation That Rewired My Brain

My body was still shaky, but a sense of calm began to settle inside me. I kept talking to myself in the mirror, like my life depended on it. Because maybe it did. "You're not a fortune teller. You're a memory machine. You can't predict John's behavior based on your ex's behavior. You can't sentence John for another person's crimes." I pressed my palms against the mirror, feeling the cool glass ground me in the present moment. "We survived that betrayal, and we're stronger now. But we won't survive sabotaging every good thing that comes our way." For the first time in my adult life, I felt a shift as my nervous system   listened. The python around my lungs loosened up a tiny bit. I walked back to the kitchen, where John was still sitting. He probably was wondering if he'd stepped on an emotional landmine.

The old story was still whispering, don't trust him, make him cancel or have him take you with him. As I leaned in to hear my thoughts, I could hear it for what it was, an echo from the past, not a prophecy about the future. "I got triggered when you mentioned Vegas," I told him directly, settling back into my chair. "Not because of anything you've done, but because of what someone else did years ago. My brain is trying to protect me by assuming the worst about you, and that's not fair to either of us." John's face softened with understanding. No defensiveness. No anger that I'd essentially accused him of future crimes. No demands that I "get over it" or "trust him." Just: "What do you need?" Those three words nearly broke me open with their gentleness. "I need you to go have fun and enjoy your time away," I said, surprising myself with the truth. "And I need to prove to myself that I can trust you completely, not because you've earned it through perfection, but because you've never given me a reason not to trust you."

The Weekend That Broke a Decades-Old Pattern

CHOOSE YOUR PATH: Path A represents the old me: I Would have spent the weekend spiraling into worst-case scenarios. I would have analyzed every text for hidden meanings, but I would have also fallen apart if he hadn't answered his phone immediately. I would have been waiting by the door when he returned, armed with accusations and suspicion.

Path B represents the healed me: I didn't spend the weekend writing tragic endings in my head. I didn't wait for the other shoe to drop. I didn't analyze his texts or panic when he left his phone off during the poker tournament. I didn't create stories about what he might be doing or who he might meet. Instead, I did something radical. I trusted. Not blind trust, conscious trust. I chose to believe in John's character, not an ex's betrayal. I decided to live in the present, not the past. I chose love over fear, even though fear felt safer and more familiar.

When John came home Sunday night with stories about terrible poker hands and overpriced drinks, he found me peacefully watching a movie on the couch. The vanilla candle was lit again, creating that same domestic peace from our morning conversation. No interrogation about where he'd been or who he'd talked to. No suspicious inspection of his phone. No punishment for having fun without me. Just a woman who'd finally learned the difference between intuition and trauma response. "How was your trip?" I asked genuinely, as I paused my movie.

"Good," he said, settling next to me with visible relief. I missed you. How was your weekend? "Peaceful," I said, surprising myself. I enjoyed having time to myself. That might sound simple, but for a woman who had spent decades interpreting solitude as a sign of abandonment, it was transformative.

The P.R.E.S.E.N.T Method: Your Anti-Trigger Protocol

The previous experience taught me a systematic approach to handling triggers, which I call the P.R.E.S.E.N.T Method, your emergency protocol for when the past tries to hijack the present.

Before we dive in, remember healing isn't linear. You won't apply this perfectly every time, and that's okay. Progress is personal, sometimes involves stepping back, and always requires compassion for yourself. You are not alone in this process.

P - PAUSE

The moment you feel triggered, stop everything. Don't act, speak, or make decisions. Just pause.

Recognizing the Trigger Signal: Your body knows before your mind does; heart racing, chest tightening, that familiar sick feeling in your stomach. Your voice changes, hands shake or go numb. You feel the urgent need to fight, flee, freeze, or fawn. This isn't a weakness; it's your nervous system working to keep you safe. Honor it, then override it.

The 5-Second Scramble: You have 5 seconds before your triggered brain decides how to respond. Don't do something you will later regret, instead:

Put down your phone, don't text or call.

Step back physically if someone is in front of you.

Put your hand on your heart this signals safety to your nervous system.

Say: "I'm triggered. This is an old pain."

Emergency Breathing, the 4-7-8: This tactical breathing physiologically calms your nervous system:

Inhale through your nose for 4 counts

Hold for 7 counts

Exhale through your mouth for 8 counts

Repeat 3 times minimum

The extended exhale activates your parasympathetic nervous system, switching you from fight-or-flight to rest-and-digest. Try this now: Take three breaths using the 4-7-8 method. Notice how even practicing when calm changes your body's state. Remember: Even a messy, imperfect pause beats a triggered reaction you'll regret.

R - RECOGNIZE the Time Warp

Triggers are like time machines. In seconds, you're not your current age, you're 12 watching a parent die, 30 being betrayed, 8 being told you're too much. Your body doesn't know the difference between then and now, but you can teach it.

Age Detection Questions:

How old does my voice sound in my head right now?

What age was I when I first felt this exact helplessness, rage, or terror?

If I had to paint this feeling, what age would I be holding the brush?

What younger version of me just took over?

Name It Specifically: Don't just say "triggered." Be precise:

"I'm 40 and just found out about the infidelity"

"I'm 12 and no one is listening"

"I'm 8 and Daddy isn't coming home"

Your Body's Timeline- Different ages live in different places:

Tight throat? The age you learned to swallow your words

Clenched fists? When you wanted to fight but couldn't

Collapsed chest? When you first felt the weight of carrying everyone

Say It Out Loud: "Right now I feel ___ years old, and I'm experiencing ___."

Then add: "That was then. This is now. I'm actually, name your current age, and I'm safe."

This isn't denial, it's differentiation. The moment you name the age; you've started separating your adult self from your triggered self. That separation is where your power lives.

E - EXAMINE Your Current Surroundings

Ground yourself in the present using the 5-4-3-2-1 Technique:

5 things you see

4 things you can touch

3 things you hear

The 37-Year Run

2 things you smell

1 thing you taste

Then say:

My name is _____.

I am ___ years old.

Today is (full date).

I am in (specific location).

I am safe because (specific evidence).

I have power now because (specific examples).

S - SEPARATE Past from Present

State the facts clearly to break the time warp.

The Separation Script:

What happened then: Specific past event

Who did it: Their name

What's happening now: Current situation

Who's here now: Current person

Why they're different: Specific evidence

Example: "My ex cheated and lied. John is not my ex. John has been transparent. John leaves his phone unlocked, and includes me, and chooses us."

The Evidence List:

Past Person | Current Person

Lied constantly | Tells hard truths

Hid phone | Shares passwords

Gaslit me | Validates feelings

Disappeared | Stays present

Broke promises | Keeps word

The Clean Slate Declaration: "I choose to respond to what is happening, not what happened."

"I see who is here, not who was here. I live in this present moment, not that past moment."

Separation isn't forgetting, it's not forcing the present self to wear the past's costume.

E - ENGAGE Your Adult Self

Ask: "What would the wisest, strongest version of me do right now?"

CEO of Your Life Questions:

What decision would make me proud in a year?

What would I advise my daughter?

What would someone who loves themselves choose?

What would courage look like here?

The Power Stance Check: Stand up straight, shoulders back, chin up, hand on heart. From this position of strength, what's your next move?

The Adult Response Menu:

Instead of running, fighting, freezing and pleasing → communicate, set a boundary, pause, and evaluate.

Instead of I can't handle this → I've handled worse and survived.

Instead of "They'll leave me → If they leave, I'll survive that too.

N - NURTURE Your Nervous System

Speak to yourself with the love you'd show a frightened child.

The Internal Mother Voice:

Not: "You're being stupid" → "Of course you're scared, what you went through was terrifying

Not: "You're overreacting" → "Your body is trying to protect you"

Not: "You should be over this" → "Healing takes time"

Physical Nurturing:

Hug yourself literally

Rock gently side to side

Stroke your arms softly

Hand on heart: "I've got you"

Wrap in a blanket

The Comfort Script: "[your name], I see how scared you are. Anyone who went through what you went through would feel this way. You're not crazy or broken. You're human. You're safe now. We've got this."

Body Comfort Checklist: ☐ Lower shoulders ☐ Unclench jaw ☐ Relax hands ☐ Lift sternum ☐ Soften eyes and smile

T - TAKE Action in The Moment

Make ONE decision based on current reality, not past trauma.

Pick ONE action:

Tell someone what you need

Take a 15-minute walk

Call a friend

Journal for 5 minutes

The Opposite Action Principle: What trauma wants → What you choose:

Isolate → Reach out to one person

Run → Stay five more minutes

Hide → Share one true thing

People please → State one need

Panic → Make one slow decision

The Victory List (write after): "I was triggered and didn't run, attack, shut down, or abandon myself." Instead, I: [what you did]

The Growth Statement: "The old me would have [old pattern]. The healing me chose [new action]. This is evidence I'm becoming [who you're becoming]."

Real-Life Examples:

Spouse comes home late → This is [spouse], not my ex. This is now, not then.

Friend doesn't text back → Sarah is busy, not abandoning me.

Being left on read → People have lives. This isn't personal.

Plans changing → Flexibility isn't rejection.

Your Personal Trigger Map

Complete these sentences:

My nervous system spikes when ….

The physical sensation I feel is ….

The voice in my head says ….

This reminds me of when ….

The 37-Year Run

The story I tell myself is ....

The person I become when triggered is ....

The person I want to be when triggered is ....

When Self-Help Isn't Enough

Sometimes triggers are too deeply rooted in trauma for self-management alone. If your triggers are overwhelming or significantly interfering with your life, seeking professional support isn't a weakness; it's wisdom. A therapist can help you navigate complex emotional patterns that require expertise beyond what any book can provide. You're not just managing triggers; you're rewriting your entire response system, one present-moment choice at a time.

The Relationship Stress Test

John and I had been married six months when out of nowhere I became triggered. It started innocently enough. John always walked through our front door, from work, at 5:15 PM. If he were to be late, he'd text. That afternoon, I messaged him about dinner. Silence. I called. Nothing. Six o'clock came and went. The house felt too quiet, as if it were holding its breath. By 6:30, my body remembered every abandonment I'd ever survived. My chest tightened like someone was sitting on it. My hands got cold. The old voices, the ones I thought I'd silenced, started their familiar chorus: Your luck finally ran out. He met someone new, or he got in a car accident and was in the hospital. At 7 PM, my fingers shook as I dialed one more time. "Hey, babe," His voice was alive. Completely unaware that I'd just spent an hour planning his funeral and our divorce simultaneously. His phone had been charging at his desk while he'd been trapped in back-to-back meetings, racing to meet a deadline he'd warned me about last week. A deadline I'd forgotten in my spiral toward catastrophe.

But here's how I knew I had healed: I didn't collapse. I didn't accuse. I didn't make him pay for crimes he hadn't committed. Instead, I used the following protocol.

PAUSE: "I'm feeling triggered by not being able to reach him."

RECOGNIZE: I feel like that scared woman again, waiting for bad news. Examine: I'm in my living room and John did mention he had a busy week. John's never lied to me.

SEPARATE: Past partners used to lie about working late. John has never given me a reason to not trust him.

ENGAGE: The strongest version of me trusts until given a reason not to.

TAKE ACTION: I will greet him with relief, not accusations.

When John walked through the door, he just hugged me and said, "I told you last week I was working late today." Instead of unleashing the anxiety that had been building, I took a breath and simply replied, "I was worried when I couldn't reach you, worried, not suspicious. There's a difference." The relief on his face said everything. I'm so thankful the unhealed version of me didn't show up to punish him for circumstances beyond his control or make him pay for another man's sins.

The Invitation Hidden in Every Trigger

Your triggers aren't just warnings; they're invitations. Invitations to choose differently from what you've done in the past. Invitations to prove you're not who you used to be. Invitations to step into the person who trusts their judgment, honors their worth, and refuses to let yesterday's pain rob tomorrow's joy. The most beautiful part about healing your triggers isn't that you stop feeling them, it's that you stop being controlled by them. John mentioning traveling solo still creates a momentary flutter of old fear, but now I recognize it immediately, "Oh, hello, old story. I see you trying to drive again. Thanks for trying to protect me, but I've got this."

Your Present Moment Is Waiting

Your past is a hijacker, waiting for the perfect moment to grab the wheel. It knows your vulnerabilities. It memorized your breaking points. It shows up dressed as logic, whispering reasonable sounding lies like this is happening again. You know how this ends. You should run now before it gets worse. But here's what took me thirty-seven years to learn: you don't have to hand over the keys anymore. Every trigger that surges through you is an opportunity to choose. Every time your chest tightens and your mind races back to old wounds, you're standing at a crossroad. Every panic attack, every emotional flashback, every moment when the past tries to convince you it's the present, these aren't defeats. They're opportunities to prove that the person who got hurt back then isn't driving anymore.

The old story will always be in the car with you. Trauma doesn't disappear; it just loses its authority to navigate. It might scream from the backseat. It might try to grab the wheel at red lights and sharp turns. But you get to decide whether to pull over and switch seats or keep your hands steady at ten and two, eyes forward, driving toward the life you're creating instead of away from the one that broke you.

Addressing Your Healing Fears

"What if I ignore a real red flag?" Trust your intuition, not your triggers. Red flags are consistent patterns of behavior, not isolated incidents. Real intuition feels calm and clear. Trauma response feels panicked and desperate. "What if trusting again leads to betrayal?" Then you'll handle it from a place of strength, not weakness. You survived betrayal despite having no tools or boundaries. Now you're equipped with self-awareness, healthy limits, and the understanding that betrayal reflects their character, not your worth. "What if my partner thinks I'm crazy for being triggered?" The right person responds with curiosity and compassion, not judgment. How someone handles your healing journey reveals everything about their character and compatibility with you.

The Freedom on the Other Side of Fear

Here's what happened when I stopped allowing my past betrayals to hijack my present love. My body relaxed. The chronic hypervigilance dissolved because I was no longer bracing for danger that wasn't coming. My relationships have deepened. When you're present, instead of protecting against phantom threats, people can reach your heart. My energy has returned. The exhausting work of scanning for betrayal was redirected toward creating genuine intimacy. My intuition sharpened. When you stop reacting to false alarms, you can hear real warning signals when they occur. Most importantly, I stopped punishing good people for the crimes of other people. John didn't have to pay for my past ex's betrayal, and my friends didn't have to prove their loyalty repeatedly because someone else had left.

CHAPTER FOUR

Breaking Free from the Lies You Tell Yourself

How Limiting Beliefs Hijack Your Life and How to Fire Them

I was hyperventilating so intensely that the car window fogged up. My hands were shaking so badly I couldn't even grip my phone to make a call. Just two miles to go, the exact route I'd driven hundreds of times without thinking. But suddenly, my own mind had turned against me, like a trusted ally gone rogue, convinced that this ordinary Tuesday errand would somehow kill me.

The panic hit the moment I pulled onto the main road, not gradually, but like a sledgehammer to the chest. It stole my breath and flooded my body with terror so pure; I was convinced I was dying. Part of me felt shame, not just fear, but shame that I was paralyzed by something as mundane as a grocery store run, something any functioning adult should handle without a second thought.

There was no danger. No threat. No rational reason for my body to think it was under attack. Just me, my car, and a simple grocery run. That's when I realized the most terrifying truth of all. I had become a prisoner in my own life, and the prison guard was made entirely of my own thoughts. Sitting there, gasping for air in a grocery store parking lot, I literally heard myself say out loud, "This is insane. I am a grown woman afraid of buying milk." And that's when something clicked. I wasn't afraid of the grocery store. I was afraid of the part of me that still believed fear meant danger, and that realization cracked something open.

Valerie Maksym

The Prison I Had Built Without Realizing It

The grocery store panic wasn't quite my rock bottom. That came three weeks later, when I realized I was afraid to answer my own front door. The familiar click of the lock had become a trigger, echoing through the foyer like an alarm every time I even thought about opening it.

My world had shrunk into a three-block radius around my house. Beyond that, my chest would start to constrict, like someone was slowly tightening a vice around my lungs. I had mapped out every bathroom between my house and necessary destinations, not because of any medical condition, but because panic made my body betray me in the most humiliating ways.

I had become a hostage negotiator with my own thoughts. Every morning, I'd wake up and start bargaining: "Okay, brain, if I promise not to try anything new today, will you let me go to the store without a panic attack?"

The escalation was gradual but devastating. In month one, I stopped driving anywhere unfamiliar. By month three I stopped driving alone. Around month six I stopped leaving my neighborhood. Soon after that, I ordered groceries online and having them delivered.

My daughter stopped asking me to go to her out-of-town dance competitions; she already knew I'd say no because I wouldn't risk driving that far alone. My friends stopped inviting me places because I always had an excuse not to go. I was watching my life shrink in real time, becoming smaller and smaller, until I feared I might disappear entirely.

The Difference Between Triggers and Prison Guards

At the time, I thought I was having a nervous breakdown. I didn't even have the words to describe what I was feeling. I knew nothing about limiting beliefs, neural pathways, or the difference between thoughts and reality. All I knew was that somehow, my own mind had become my enemy.

Years would pass before I could connect the dots, before I understood that this parking lot breakdown was different from the trigger work, I'd previously worked on. This wasn't about past trauma hijacking the present. It was something deeper, more deceptive.

Triggers are external; they are situations that activate old wounds. But limiting beliefs? They're the prison guards that live in your mind 24/7, constantly scanning for reasons why you can't, shouldn't, or aren't allowed to live freely.

The trigger needed John to mention Vegas to activate. The prison guard didn't need a reason; it was always on duty. Always ready to shut down my dreams, limit my choices, and keep me small.

This wasn't about what someone had done to me. This was about what I had done to myself, through decades of toxic self-talk, catastrophic thinking, and limiting beliefs that had hardened into invisible prison walls.

The Voices That Built My Prison

Dr. Daniel Siegel's research revealed something that finally made sense of my torment. I wasn't just thinking negative thoughts; I was literally rewiring my brain for captivity. Every time I obeyed a limiting belief, I was strengthening the neural pathways that kept me small. I was becoming an architect of my own mental prison.

Sitting in that parking lot, tears streaming down my face, I finally heard them clearly, the chorus of voices that had been running my life from the shadows.

My ex's voice: *"You're too much. You can't handle real pressure. Look how you're falling apart over nothing."*

My mother's voice: "No. Period. Because I said so. Growing up, it was common for adults to say, 'Kids are meant to be seen, not heard.

My childhood voice: "If you stay small and don't ask for much, maybe no one will hurt you or leave you."

Society's voice: "Women your age should be grateful for whatever they get. Stop wanting so much."

And my own voice, the cruelest of all: "Who do you think you are, trying to start a public speaking and coaching business? You couldn't even handle grocery shopping without falling apart. Stick to what you know before you embarrass yourself publicly."

These weren't just thoughts. They had become my internal operating system, the unquestioned rules that governed every decision, every dream, every possibility I allowed myself to consider.

The Voices That Built My Prison

As I got better at recognizing my internal prison guard, I started collecting its favorite phrases, each one disguised as protection but rooted in fear.

The Safety Warden: "Don't try anything new. Remember what happened last time. You'll just get hurt again."
What lesson about courage might be hidden here?

The Inadequacy Inspector: "Everyone else is more qualified. You'll embarrass yourself. They'll see right through you."
Could this be prompting you to embrace vulnerability and growth?

The Age Auditor: "You're too old to start over. That ship has sailed. Accept your lot in life."
What insight could be waiting beneath this fear?

The Perfectionist Police: *"If you can't do it perfectly, don't do it at all. Mediocrity is worse than not trying."*
How can I find strength in progress over perfection?

The Scarcity Sheriff: *"There's not enough time, money, or opportunity for people like you. The good stuff goes to other people."*
What path toward abundance could this be revealing?

The Comparison Captain: *"Look at what she accomplished at your age. You'll never measure up. You missed your chance."*
Is this a sign to celebrate my unique journey instead of imitating others?

Each of these voices felt protective, like they were trying to save me from disappointment or failure. But protection that keeps you from living isn't protection; it's imprisonment.

The B.E.L.I.E.F System: Breaking Mental Prisons

After being held hostage by my own mind, I developed what I call the B.E.L.I.E.F System, a six-step method for identifying and dismantling the limiting beliefs that imprison you.

B - BECOME Aware of the Prison Guard's Voice

Notice when limiting thoughts arise. The prison guard's common phrases:

"I can't handle this."

"I'm not strong enough."

"Something bad will happen."

"I don't deserve this."

"This is too hard."

"People like me don't..."

"I'll probably fail anyway."

"I should be realistic."

E - **EXAMINE** the Evidence

Is this thought true, or is it just familiar?

Has this fear ever actually materialized?

What evidence contradicts this belief?

When have I handled difficult things successfully?

Am I treating fears like facts?

L - **LOCATE** the Origin

Where did this belief come from? A critical parent who projected their fears onto you? A past failure that you generalized into a life sentence? A cruel teacher who crushed your confidence? Have you accepted someone else's limitations as your own?

I- **INTERRUPT** the Pattern

The moment you notice the limiting thought, tell yourself, "That's my prison guard talking, not reality." Call it what it is, a thought, not a truth. Recognize the voice as outdated protection and refuse to automatically obey its commands.

E - **EXCHANGE** the Lie for Truth

Replace the limiting belief with evidence-based reality. "I can't handle this" becomes "I've handled difficult things before and can learn what I don't know." "I'm not strong enough" becomes "I'm stronger than I realize and can build the strength I need." "I always fail at everything" becomes "I've succeeded at things that mattered to me." "I'm too old" becomes "I have experience and wisdom that younger people don't have."

The 37-Year Run

F - FIND Evidence of Your Capability

Take one action that contradicts old beliefs, even if it scares you. Go after the job or career, your limiting beliefs say you'll never have. Sign up for the class your inner critic says you missed your chance for. Begin the project that fear says you're not qualified to do.

The Grocery Store Prison Break

The day in the parking lot became the 6-step blueprint for how I'd face the prison guard that tried to keep me playing small in the comfort of my home.

Step One: Awareness
This is my anxiety talking, not reality. I hear the prison guard trying to keep me home.

Step Two: Examine the Evidence
What proof do I have that driving to the grocery store is dangerous? None. I've driven this route hundreds of times safely.

Step Three: Locate the Origin
This fear traces back to my father's sudden death when I was twelve, when I learned that normal moments could turn into disasters without warning.

Step Four: Interrupt the Pattern

That was then. This is now. That was a medical emergency. This is a grocery run. I am not my twelve-year-old self.

Step Five: Exchange the Lie
I am not powerless or fragile. I am a capable adult who drives safely every day.

Step Six: Find New Evidence

I will sit in this car for five more minutes, then drive to the store and buy groceries like the competent woman I am.

It wasn't magical. My hands were still shaking as I put the car in drive. But for the first time in months, I refused to let the prison guard make decisions on my behalf.

Your Prison Guard Audit

Right now, as you read this, your own prison guard might be whispering, "This worked for her, but your situation is different. Your limitations are real." That voice? That's exactly what I'm talking about. That's the enemy. The liar that's been running your life, stealing your dreams, and convincing you that your cage is actually safety. It's time to challenge that voice. Take this audit to identify the limiting beliefs that have built your personal prison.

Complete these sentences:

"I could never..."

"I'm not the type of person who..."

"People like me don't..."

"It's too late for me to..."

"I don't have what it takes to..."

Now ask yourself:

Where did these beliefs come from?

What evidence supports them?

What evidence contradicts them?

How have these beliefs limited my choices?

The 37-Year Run

What would I attempt if I knew these thoughts were lies?

The beliefs that feel most true are often the ones holding you most captive.

The Compound Effect of Mental Freedom

Here's what happened when I stopped obeying my internal prison guard:

My world has expanded. Opportunities I'd never noticed before became visible, because I was no longer filtering them out as "not for me."

My energy has increased. The exhausting work of constant self-limitation was finally redirected toward real goals.

My relationships have improved. When you stop limiting yourself, you stop limiting what you can offer others.

My dreams have come true. Goals I'd buried under "realistic thinking" came back to life.

Most importantly, I stopped being my own worst enemy.

The voice that had spent decades explaining why I couldn't became the voice that started figuring out how I could.

The Truth That Sets You Free

The woman who couldn't drive two miles to the grocery store wasn't sick or broken. She believed her thoughts were nothing more than lies. And the same might be true for you. Your limiting beliefs aren't protecting you; they're imprisoning you.

Every "I can't" is another bar in your cage. Every "I'm not

good enough" is another lock on your door. But here's the liberating truth that day in the parking lot taught me. You are both the prisoner and the guard. Which means you hold the key.

The question isn't whether you can overcome your limiting beliefs. The question is: How much longer will you let the prison guard run your life? The woman sobbing in that parking lot thought her limitations were real, too. She was wrong. And so are you.

Your prison break begins the moment you stop believing every thought that crosses your mind.

Stop obeying the prison guard.

Start questioning its authority.

Stop treating fears like facts.

Start treating courage as a choice.

Stop accepting limitations as permanent.

Start seeing them as suggestions you're allowed to decline.

The life you want is waiting on the other side of the beliefs that say you can't have it.
It's time to prove your prison guard wrong. Before you turn the page, choose one belief that's been limiting your possibilities, and decide to test whether it's true. This single moment of courage can ignite your transformation. Change doesn't begin with perfection; it begins with one brave choice, the choice to challenge a belief that's been holding you back. The choice to ask, "What if this isn't true?" The choice to take one small step in the direction of freedom, even if your hands are still shaking.

CHAPTER FIVE

Walls Don't Protect, They Imprison
Emotional Barriers Keep Love Out

After months of unloading other people's baggage, learning to exist authentically, managing my triggers, and firing the prison guard, I thought I had cracked the code on healing. I could drive to the grocery store without a panic attack. I could voice my preferences instead of disappearing into "I don't care." I was making real progress. Then came the text that shattered my illusion of transformation. I was sitting alone at another social event, safely invisible in the back corner, when my phone lit up with a message that would haunt me for years: "I can't do this anymore, Valerie. I've tried to love you, but it's like loving a ghost. You're there, but you're never really present." As I read those words, a cold shiver ran through me. The smell of stale coffee hung in the air, bitter and cold, like everything else in my life had become.

The text was from my best friend of five years; the woman I called my sister. The person I thought understood me better than anyone. The friend I loved so deeply, I would have done anything for her, except, apparently, let her love me back. That message came right after my second divorce, during a time when my world was already crumbling, and I needed her most. Instead of support, I got silence. Instead of comfort, I got abandoned.

At first, I was angry. How could she leave me at my lowest point? How could someone who claimed to love me like family disappear when I needed her most? It took me years to understand the devastating truth. She didn't leave because she stopped caring. She left because loving someone who hides behind impenetrable walls had exhausted her beyond repair. Though it was a moment of intense heartache, it became a turning point, an unexpected invitation to reassess and reconstruct my life with honesty. Over time, I discovered something powerful: Every significant loss carries the potential for major growth. Every heartbreak holds the possibility of healing. And every ending can become the beginning of a wiser, more open version of yourself.

Why Emotional Walls Feel Safe-But Keep You Lonely

What I didn't know at the time was that I was experiencing emotional numbing, a trauma response where the brain shuts down its ability to feel pain. That realization gave painful clarity to my best friend's words.

Brené Brown's research on vulnerability helped me understand what was really happening. When we armor ourselves against hurt, we don't just block pain; we also block love, joy, and connection.

So, what takes place in the brain when we build emotional walls?

The **e**mpathy center becomes less active, making it harder to connect with others emotionally. It's like sitting across from a friend who's crying during a movie and wondering why you feel nothing.

The **t**hinking brain overrides emotional responses, leading to a flat effect. You're present, but not emotionally available, watching life through glass.

The resonance circuits that help us feel with others fire less frequently. This makes people feel like they can't reach you. You might miss a friend's emotional cue at dinner simply because your mind is elsewhere.

The 37-Year Run

People who build high emotional walls may experience:

More relationship breakdowns.

Increased loneliness, even when surrounded by others.

Difficulty forming deep connections.

A constant feeling of being misunderstood.

The cruel irony is this: The protection that keeps pain out also keeps love out.

The Moment I Started Building Walls

The wall that would eventually cost me my best friend began construction on the worst night of my childhood. I was twelve, lying next to my dying father, listening to him talk about angels and bright lights while I tried desperately to understand every word. When he collapsed in the hallway bathroom, his body turned purple, and I stood frozen in terror. In that moment, something inside me made a decision that would shape the next four decades of my life. I will never ever be that helpless and heartbroken again. The twelve-year-old who watched her father die didn't just lose a parent that night. She lost her faith in forever. Her trust in love. Her belief that people stay. In that moment of unbearable pain, she began building walls around her heart, brick by brick.

The first wall was silence. I stopped talking about feelings because they hurt too much.

The second wall was detachment. I learned to care, but not too much; to love, but not too deeply.

The third wall was observation. I became an expert at watching other people's lives instead of fully living my own.

The fourth wall was performance. I became an indispensable helper, fixing everyone else's problems so they wouldn't look too closely at mine.

By the time I met a best friend, in my forties, I had built an emotional fortress so sophisticated, even I believed it was home.

Reflecting on my own story, I invite you to consider the first wall you put up. Was there a moment when pain or loss made vulnerability feel too risky? We all have those turning points when protection becomes isolation.

As you reflect, ask yourself: Are those walls still standing? Are they still shaping your relationships, your choices, and your ability to connect? And most importantly, what steps can you take to begin gently dismantling them?

The W.A.L.L. Method- Recognizing Emotional Barriers

Building on these realizations from my story and working with clients, I've identified four types of emotional walls that keep us trapped in ghost-like relationships.

W - WITHDRAWAL

Picture this: I'm mid-conversation, the topic grows personal, and suddenly, I'm excusing myself to check on something trivial in the other room. I would pull back when conversations got deep, change subjects when emotions arose, or physically remove myself when vulnerability was required. My best friend's complaint. "Every time I try to have a real conversation with you, you find a way to disappear."

A – ANALYSIS

Imagine you're sharing something deeply personal, and instead of empathy, you receive a breakdown of why you feel that way, as if it's a puzzle to solve. You intellectualize emotions instead of feeling them, turning everything into a problem to solve rather than an experience to share. My best friend's frustration, you analyze my feelings like a therapist instead of connecting with me like a friend.

L - LIGHTHEARTEDNESS

Think about those moments when someone opens up about their struggles, and instead of leaning in, you deflect with a joke, trying to lighten the mood but unintentionally creating distance. You avoid serious conversations with humor, crack jokes when others are being vulnerable, or steer things away when they start to feel too heavy. I'll never forget my best friend's observation. "I can't share anything difficult with you because you immediately try to make things lighter instead of just being with me in it." That sentence hit hard. Because she wasn't asking for solutions or laughter, she was asking me to be present, to be with her in the moment.

L – LOGISTICS

Visualize a friend confiding in you about personal issues, and you respond with something off topic like suggesting a new project to work on together. You focus on practical matters to avoid emotional ones, offering solutions when people need support, or talking about tasks when they want to talk about emotions and feelings.

The Performance Review That Shattered Everything

Three months after losing my best friend, my life coach gave me an exercise that exposed the full extent of my emotional imprisonment. "Describe your closest relationship," she said. "But only talk about how you feel in it, not what you do for them." I sat in silence for what felt like fifteen minutes. As I tried to connect with my feelings, my chest tightened, and my throat constricted, a physical reminder of the emotional void inside me. I could list everything I did for my closest friendship in my life: the gifts I bought, the favors I performed, the problems I solved. But I couldn't describe the feeling I experienced in their presence. That's when I understood the difference between performing love and feeling love. I had become such a master performer that even I believed the show was real. I thought being useful was the same as being connected. I thought showing up was the same as being present. I thought caring about someone was the same as letting them care about me.

Brené Brown's research on vulnerability helped me make sense of it. People who struggle with emotional intimacy often confuse proximity with connection. You can be physically present but emotionally absent, creating relationships that look functional but feel hollow. I invite you to try the same exercise: Choose one of your closest relationships and describe the relationship only through the lens of your emotions, not your actions. How do you feel when you're with them? Are those feelings different from what you show? This reflection can reveal powerful insights about the depth and authenticity of your connections and may be the first step toward building relationships rooted in emotional truth, not performance.

The Three-Step Wall Demolition Process

After losing my best friend and recognizing a recurring emotional pattern, I developed a 3-step systematic approach to dismantling the walls I had built around my feelings.

Step 1: The Daily Feeling Check

Three times a day, ask yourself: *"What am I feeling right now?"* Not thinking, feeling. Name the emotion specifically. It sounds simple, but after decades of emotional numbing, I realized I could only identify three feelings: fine, tired, and stressed. I had to relearn my emotional vocabulary.

I remember the first time I truly paid attention during a daily feeling check. I was standing at the kitchen counter when I realized I was anxious, not tired. That small victory created a ripple effect, encouraging me to keep going and to trust the process of genuinely connecting with my emotions.

Step 2: The Vulnerability Practice

Share one authentic feeling with one person every day. Start small.

"I'm nervous about this meeting."

"That comment hurt my feelings."

"I'm excited about this weekend."

"I feel lonely when you're traveling."

"I feel so happy spending time with you."

Step 3: The Presence Commitment

When someone shares something vulnerable with you, resist the urge to fix, analyze, or deflect. Just be with them in their experience. Say things like:

"That sounds really hard."

"I can see why you'd feel that way."

"Thank you for trusting me with this."

The Friend Who Broke Through My Walls

Two years into my wall demolition project, I met a new girlfriend. But this time, when she started getting close, instead of retreating behind my usual defenses, I did something terrifying, I let her see my mess. When she asked how I was doing, I told her the truth instead of performing. When she opened up emotionally, I responded with honesty instead of deflecting solutions. When she expressed how much she valued our friendship, I practiced saying it back and meaning it. The transformation was immediate and profound. For the first time in my adult life, I felt the deep, soul-level connection I had been craving but had been too afraid to create. The difference wasn't that she was easier to talk to or that I was better at showing gratitude. The difference was that I had finally become someone who allowed myself to be loved. I recognize that not everyone has a friend like this in their life. If that's the case for you, consider keeping a journal to express your deepest thoughts and feelings, allowing yourself to be seen on paper. Alternatively, seek out communities on platforms that prioritize emotional safety, where you can share and connect with others on similar journeys, even when face-to-face interaction isn't possible.

The Letter I Never Sent

Five years after our friendship ended, I wrote a letter to my former best friend that I had never sent.

You were right about everything. I was a ghost, present, but not really there. You tried to love someone who wouldn't let herself be known, and that's not love, that's performance art. I spent five years giving you everything except the one thing you asked for: the real me. I was so busy protecting myself from being hurt again that I made it impossible for you to love me. You didn't abandon me. I abandoned myself so completely that there was no one left for you to connect with.

Thank you for trying as long as you did. Thank you for seeing that there was someone worth knowing behind all those walls, even when I couldn't see her myself. You taught me that walls don't just keep people out, they keep you locked in. And life begins the moment you choose connection over protection.

The 37-Year Run

The Neuroscience of Emotional Availability

According to Dr. Daniel Siegel's research, consistent emotional vulnerability leads to measurable changes in the brain. Three key areas begin to transform:

The insula, which governs emotional awareness, becomes more active, helping you better identify and name your feelings.

The anterior cingulate cortex strengthens, enhancing your capacity for empathy and emotional attunement.

The prefrontal cortex learns to regulate emotions, not by suppressing them, but by integrating them.

In other words, emotional availability isn't just about willpower; it's about rewiring your brain for connection.

Your Ghost Assessment

Ask yourself these uncomfortable questions:

Do people say you're "hard to read"?

Do friends complain that you don't share your feelings enough or seem distant?

Do you deflect compliments, change the subject when conversations get deep, or find reasons to leave when emotions arise?

Are you more comfortable giving support than receiving it?

Do you feel lonely even when surrounded by people who care about you?

Have people described loving you as "exhausting" or "one-sided"?

If you answered yes to three or more, you might be unintentionally hurting your own relationships.

The 21-Day Emotional Resurrection Challenge

Week 1: Feel

Set three alarms each day. When they go off, pause and name one emotion you're experiencing, out loud. Together, we'll expand our emotional vocabulary beyond just fine, tired, and stressed. This is still an ongoing practice for me, too, as I continue learning to recognize and articulate my feelings more clearly.

Week 2: Share

Each day, share one genuine emotion with one person. I'll be doing this alongside you. We'll start with low-stakes feelings like excitement, gratitude, mild frustration, or anticipation, building trust in ourselves and others through small, honest moments.

Week 3: Stay

When someone shares something personal, resist the urge to fix, analyze, or change the subject. Let's support each other in staying present with others in their emotional experiences, offering connection instead of control.

As you resist the urge to fix, analyze, or change the subject when someone shares something vulnerable, I'll do the same. We can support each other by staying present with others in their experiences.

The Advanced Connection Protocol

As you grow in emotional availability, you can begin practicing more advanced techniques to deepen your relationships:

The Mirror Exercise: When someone shares a feeling, reflect it back before responding. For example, if a friend says, "I'm so stressed from work lately," you might reply, "It sounds like you're feeling overwhelmed by everything going on at work." This kind of live dialogue offers a practical way to rehearse emotional presence and validation.

The Permission Practice: Before offering advice, ask, "Do you want me to listen, or do you want solutions?" This simple question honors the other person's needs and prevents unintentional emotional bypassing.

The Matching Method: When someone opens up vulnerably, meet them at their level of openness. Resist the urge to retreat into emotional safety; connection thrives in mutual vulnerability.

The Check-In Commitment: Begin conversations with, "How are you really doing?" instead of defaulting to surface-level pleasantries. This invites authenticity and shows you're truly present.

The Connection That's Waiting

The deep, soul-level friendships you've longed for are waiting, just beyond the walls you've built. A genuine connection can't happen while you're hiding behind emotional armor. The best friend in your life, the one trying to love you through those walls, might be growing weary of loving a ghost. Don't lose them the way I lost my best friend. Don't wait until someone walks away to realize you were never fully present.

Today, I have the friendships I once only dreamed of. I can share real struggles, celebrate victories, and show up authentically, even when it's messy. The difference isn't that my new friends are better than my former best friend; it's that I became someone capable of being truly known.

Your people are out there, waiting for someone brave enough to:

Communicate honestly, not perfectly.

Stay present during hard conversations.

Share their authentic self, not a curated version.

Fight for connection instead of running from it.

Stop protecting themselves from love and start opening up to it.

The real you, the messy, vulnerable, beautiful human you are, is worth knowing. But first, you must be willing to be known. Who might notice when you finally step out of hiding? Your walls aren't keeping you safe. They're keeping you alone. It's time to tear them down and return to your beautiful life.

And if this journey ever feels too daunting, remember seeking professional support is a courageous step. Therapists and counselors can offer guidance and tools to help you navigate these deeply rooted challenges. You don't have to do this alone.

CHAPTER SIX

The Friendship Assassin

How I Learned the Difference Between Performing Connection and Creating It

I was standing in my mother's modest Texas home when my childhood friend, visiting from out of town, looked around with visible confusion. Then she asked the question that marked the beginning of the end of a decade-long friendship I had cherished: *"Is this the big house you told me about?"* Her words hit me like a punch to the chest. The lie I'd told her as a kid, that I lived in a big house in Texas, suddenly felt like a weight I couldn't carry. My throat went dry, my palms began to sweat, and I felt that familiar panic of being caught in a performance I could no longer sustain.

I made up that story years ago, hoping to feel important, wanting to impress the girl who had become like family during those magical summers on my grandparents' street in Michigan. And now, here she was, standing in the modest house that had always been our only home, slowly realizing the truth: I had lied to her for years. "No," I said quickly, my voice barely above a whisper. "This is the only house."

That was it. No explanation. No apology. No admission that I had deceived someone I deeply cared about, all because I was insecure and wanted to seem special. I couldn't bring myself to say, "I made that up because I was embarrassed about where I really lived," or "I'm sorry I lied to you; I was just a kid trying to impress you." Instead, shame crept up my neck, turning my face red, and I did what I had learned to do best: I started pulling away.

From that moment on, I began to slowly dismantle our friendship. Not because we weren't compatible; we were perfect together. Not because we didn't care; our bond had been unbreakable for years. I destroyed it because I was too afraid to have one honest conversation about a childhood lie that, in the end, probably wouldn't have mattered to her at all. But that moment wasn't the end; it was the beginning. The start of a painful pattern that would eventually cost me several of the deepest friendships of my life.

The Graveyard I Built with My Own Hands

I thought I had finally mastered the art of authentic relationships. After years of deep inner healing and painful but necessary conversations with my children about the impact of my unhealed trauma, I learned to speak honestly about my mistakes. I could take accountability without defensiveness. I was building a real connection where chaos had once ruled. But behind me lay a graveyard of friendships, extraordinary women who had loved me like family, only to walk away, worn down by my inability to let them truly know me.

My out-of-town friend was the first casualty in a war I'd waged against intimacy for thirty-seven years. Woman entered my life with open hearts and genuine care. Good women. Safe women. Women who saw something in me worth loving. And I systematically destroyed every one of those friendships, not with cruelty or conflict, but with something far more insidious: performance. I gave them a carefully edited version of myself, a highlight reel where every response was calculated, every story curated, every emotion filtered through the lens of what I thought they wanted to see.

The 37-Year Run

They thought they were getting to know me. They were getting to know a ghost. You can only perform intimacy for so long before people feel the emptiness behind it. One by one, these friendships died from starvation, starved of the authenticity that makes relationships real, starved of the vulnerability that makes connection possible. I killed them with politeness, suffocated them with perfection, watched them wither while I stood behind my mask wondering why I felt so alone. The tragedy wasn't that I lost friends. The tragedy was that they never got to meet me.

The Drill Team Friend: The Art of Disappearing

We spent summers dreaming and laughing, building the kind of bond every teenage girl craves. She was my person until the day that changed everything. I can still see the list posted on the gymnasium wall; girls clustered around it, excited or devastated. Her name was on the list in neat black letters. Mine wasn't. She made the drill team; I didn't. I stood there, staring at that list, feeling the familiar burn of shame creeping up my neck. I could hear her calling my name across the gym, I could see her face light up when she spotted me. But instead of running to her, I turned and walked away. I never told her I was disappointed. I never shared my fear of being left behind. I never gave her the chance to prove that our friendship mattered more than a stupid drill team. Instead, I just stopped showing up. I watched from a distance as she moved into the popular crowd while I isolated myself, convinced my failure made me unworthy of her friendship. She never rejected me. I rejected myself and took our friendship down with it. The last time I saw her, she cornered me in the hallway. "What happened to us?" She asked, her eyes filled with confusion and hurt. "Did I do something wrong?" I could have saved our friendship with three sentences: "I didn't make the drill team. I was embarrassed and scared you'd leave me behind. I'm sorry for disappearing." Instead, I shrugged and said, "Nothing happened. We just grew apart." I watched her face crumble as she realized I wasn't going to fight for us. That was the moment I learned that sometimes the worst lies aren't the ones you tell; they're the truths you refuse to speak.

The Workout Sister: When Silence Becomes a Weapon

Years later, I found another woman, whom I called "sister," a gym partner who became my closest confidante. We'd meet every morning at 9 AM, sweating through workouts and life problems with equal intensity. She knew my coffee order, my worst fears, and my biggest dreams. When she went through a difficult divorce, I watched her begin to withdraw from everyone, including me. Our morning workouts became sporadic, then stopped altogether. Her texts went from daily check-ins to radio silence. I knew she was drowning, but instead of fighting for a friendship that had meant everything to both of us, I matched her silence with my own. I told myself I was giving her space. I convinced myself she'd reach out when she was ready. The truth? I created a pattern of mirroring others to avoid rocking the boat. In doing so, I never showed the authentic version of myself. I was terrified of saying the wrong thing or being rejected if I pushed too hard. I never persisted. Never showed up at her door. Never sent the text that said, "I'm not going anywhere, even if you push me away." I let pride and performance dictate my response instead of love and authentic connection. The last time I saw her was at the store two years later. We exchanged awkward pleasantries, both of us pretending we hadn't once been sisters. As I watched her walk away, I realized I'd let fear kill another relationship that could have lasted a lifetime.

The 37-Year Run

When Connection Becomes a Performance

At the time, I didn't realize I was trapped in what psychologists call impression management, the unconscious habit of controlling how others perceive you, rather than allowing them to truly know you. I wasn't building a connection; I was performing it. Research shows that people who consistently perform connection rather than create it tend to follow predictable patterns:

They report significantly higher rates of loneliness, even with a wide social circle, because surface-level relationships fail to meet deep emotional needs.

They experience chronic anxiety about being "found out" as less than their carefully curated persona.

They struggle to receive authentic love, believing it's the performance, not the real person, that others care about.

In relationships built on performance instead of presence, the authentic self goes into hiding to protect the curated version from being exposed as flawed. Vulnerability feels dangerous, intimacy becomes impossible, and connection slowly fades as the gap between the real person and their persona widens. Avoiding difficult conversations only accelerates this breakdown. Relationships don't fail because people don't care; they fail because they never learn how to navigate the truth together. I was living proof of this. Every friendship I'd lost had followed the same pattern. I loved these women deeply, but I never let them love the real me back.

The Isolation Behind the Image

By my forties, I had perfected the art of being loved for someone I wasn't. People constantly told me how "put together" I was, how "strong" I seemed, how I "never seemed to struggle with anything." But those compliments felt incredibly uncomfortable. They were praising a version of me that didn't exist, a carefully curated performance I had maintained for so long, I'd nearly forgotten who I was underneath it all.

The more successful the performance became, the more isolated I felt. There's a specific kind of loneliness that comes from being surrounded by people who love your act but have never met your authentic self. It's the kind of realization that if you died tomorrow, people would mourn someone who never really existed.

I would lie awake at night, chest tight with anxiety, wondering what would happen if I stopped performing. Would anyone stick around if they saw my mess? Would anyone love me if they knew how insecure, needy, and confused I actually was? The fear of being truly known had grown larger than my desire for genuine connection. So, I kept choosing the safety of surface-level relationships over the risk of deep, authentic love.

The Relationship That Changed Everything

The breakthrough didn't come through a girlfriend; it came through my husband, John. For the first time in my life, I made a radical decision: I would show up as my authentic self from day one and see what happened. No more guessing what someone wanted to hear. No more disappearing into a performance. Just me. On our first date, I let him choose the meeting spot. After our first date when he asked where I wanted to go for dinner after our first date, I told him, rather than defaulting to "I don't care." When he asked for my opinion, I gave it honestly, instead of trying to mirror his views. When he showed interest in me, I didn't shrink into gratitude, I stayed present to ask myself if I was truly interested in him too.

The most revolutionary part wasn't that he was falling in love with me. It was that, for the first time, there was a me there to be loved. I remember the first time we disagreed. In the past, I would have backed down immediately, apologized for having a different opinion, and spent the rest of the evening trying to smooth things over. But this time, I took a deep breath and said, "I see this differently than you do, and I'd like to explain why." My heart was pounding. My hands were shaking. Every instinct screamed at me to take it back, laugh it off, return to the safety of agreement. But I stayed. I shared my perspective, then I listened to his perspective on the topic. We discussed it, two adults who respected each other enough to disagree honestly. And something miraculous happened: our relationship grew stronger.

With John, I learned how to have hard conversations without shutting down. When something bothers me, I say it directly instead of hoping he'll read my mind. When I'm hurt, scared, or confused, I use my words instead of silence. When we disagree, I stay engaged instead of pretending to agree. The result? For the first time in my life, I have a relationship built on two real people choosing each other, not two performances trying to maintain an illusion.

The C.O.N.N.E.C.T. Method: Turning Performance into Presence

After losing several close friendships because I didn't know how to communicate authentically, I developed what I now call the C.O.N.N.E.C.T Method, a framework for building genuine relationships rooted in presence, not performance.

C – Catch Yourself Performing
Start by noticing when you're giving the "right" response instead of the real one. Common signs of performance include:

Saying what you think they want to hear.

Avoiding topics that might lead to conflict.

Deflecting personal questions with humor.

Focusing on their problems to avoid sharing your own.

Mentally rehearsing conversations before they happen.

Feeling drained after social interactions.

O – Open with Vulnerability
Share something true about what you're feeling or experiencing, even if it's uncomfortable:

"I'm scared you'll think less of me if I tell you this…"

"I've been pretending I'm fine, but I'm actually struggling with…"

"I was hurt when you said that, even though I laughed it off."

N – Name the Fear
Identify what you're afraid will happen if you stop performing:

"I'm afraid you'll leave if you see how needy I am."

"I'm scared you won't like the real me."

"I worry that being honest will create conflict."

N – Navigate the Discomfort
Stay present when things get uncomfortable and resist the urge to deflect or change the subject. Try saying:

"This is hard for me to talk about, but…"

"I want to tell you something that scares me."

"Can we sit with this awkward moment instead of rushing past it?"

E – Express Your Authentic Self
Let your real thoughts, feelings, and reactions come through instead of the polished version:

Share your actual opinions, not just agreeable ones.

Express excitement about things that matter to you.

The 37-Year Run

Admit it when you don't know something.

Show your messy emotions, not just the tidy ones.

C – Create Safety for Truth
Make it safe for others to be real with you by being real first:

"I want you to feel like you can tell me anything."

"I'd rather you be honest than polite with me."

"Thank you for trusting me with your real feelings."

T – Trust the Process
Believe that authentic connection is worth the risk of being truly known, even if it means some people won't stay. The ones who do will love you, not your performance.

The 93/7 Rule: Why Words Aren't Enough

Research shows that 93% of communication effectiveness comes from nonverbal cues and tone of voice, while only 7% comes from the actual words we say. This helped me understand why so many of my friendships kept falling apart, despite my best intentions.

My words said, *"I care about you."* But my tone said, *"Don't dig deeper."* My body language said, *"I'm not really here."* My energy said, *"I'm performing care, not feeling it."* My silence said, *"Your feelings aren't worth discussing."*

No wonder those incredible women eventually walked away. I wasn't giving them a real person to connect with; I was giving them a performance. And you can't build lasting intimacy with someone who's always putting on a show.

The Friendship That Met Me Where I Was

Two years into practicing authentic communication, I met a new friend. But this time, when she started getting close, I didn't retreat behind my usual performance. I did something terrifying; I let her see my mess. We were having coffee when she asked the kind of question that used to send me straight into performance mode: "How are you really doing?" Instead of my usual, "Great! Everything's wonderful!" I took a breath and told her the truth: "Honestly? I'm struggling. I'm scared about this new business I'm starting. I am going to have to get out of my comfort zone and make videos. And I feel like I'm pretending to have it all together when really I'm just figuring it out as I go." I watched her face, bracing for the polite smile and subject change I'd come to expect whenever I shared something real. But instead, her eyes lit up. "Oh, my goodness, thank you for saying that. I thought I was the only one who felt like they were making it up as they went along." When she shared something vulnerable, I didn't deflect with advice or humor; I matched her openness. When she said she cared about me, I practiced saying it back and meaning it. The transformation was immediate and profound. For the first time in my adult life, I experienced the deep, soul-level friendship I had always craved, but had been too afraid to create.

Are You Connecting or Performing?

Research shows that people who learn to communicate vulnerably experience profound shifts in their relationships and emotional well-being. According to studies by Dr. Kristin Neff, those who embrace authentic communication report:

A 42% reduction in loneliness within six months, even with fewer total social contacts.

Deeper, more meaningful relationships with the people who remain in their lives.

Greater self-acceptance, as they stop hiding their true self.

Stronger emotional resilience, thanks to genuine support systems instead of surface-level connections.

The 37-Year Run

But here's the most important insight: Transformation begins the moment you stop managing impressions and start sharing authentically.

Your Performance Assessment

Ask yourself these uncomfortable but revealing questions:

Do you often say what you think people want to hear?

Do you avoid sharing real opinions if they might cause conflict?

Are you more comfortable talking about others than revealing yourself?

Do you deflect compliments or deep questions with humor?

Have people described you as "hard to read" or "always put together"?

Have you lost friendships without ever having a real conversation about what went wrong?

Do you feel exhausted after social interactions from trying to be "on"?

Do you mentally rehearse conversations before having them?

If you answered yes to three or more, you may be performing connections instead of creating them.

The Letter That Set Me Free

A few years ago, during a quiet journaling moment, I wrote a letter I never intended to send to the out-of-state friend whose innocent question about the "big house" had triggered decades of performance-based friendships.

"You probably don't even remember asking about the big house, but I've carried that moment for thirty years. Not because you judged me for lying, but because I was too afraid to admit I made up a story to impress you. I spent our entire friendship performing the version of myself I thought you'd love, instead of trusting you to love the real me. I was so busy managing your impression of me that I never learned how to simply be with you. You deserved a friend who could be honest about silly childhood lies. You deserved someone who would fight for our friendship instead of disappearing when things got messy. You deserved the real me, not the performance I put on for you. I can't get back what we had, but I can make sure I never lose another relationship because I'm too scared to be truly known."

Writing that letter didn't bring back our friendship, but it did something even more important. It freed me from the shame that had been driving my performances for three decades. It marked the beginning of a new chapter, one where I choose truth over perfection, presence over performance, and connection over control.

The Friendships Still Waiting for You

The deep, soul-level friendships you've been craving your whole life are waiting, but not on the other side of perfection. They're waiting on the other side of your performance. Because they can't connect with your act, they need to connect with you.

Your people are out there, hoping to meet someone brave enough to:

Communicate honestly instead of perfectly.

Stay present during difficult conversations.

Share their real self instead of a curated version.

Fight for connection instead of running when things get complicated.

Looking back, I realize the out-of-town friend probably wouldn't have cared about my childhood lie, if I'd just had the

The 37-Year Run

courage to apologize. The drill team friend likely would've supported me through disappointment, if I'd shared my feelings instead of disappearing. I can't get back the friendships I lost to performance. But I can make sure I never lose another relationship because I'm too scared to let someone truly know me. Today, I'm intentionally building the kind of friendships I once only dreamed of. I share real struggles. I celebrate others' victories authentically. I come as I am when you need me. The difference isn't that my new friends are better, it's that I finally learned the difference between performing love and loving unconditionally.

Stop performing relationships, start living them. The truth I learned too late: the right people don't want your highlight reel. They want your blooper reel, your deleted scenes, the moments you'd rather edit out. They don't love you despite your mess; they love you because you trust them enough to show it. Here's what thirty-seven years of hiding taught me: every filtered response, every curated story, every time you choose perfection over truth, you're building a wall between you and the love you're desperate to feel.

CHAPTER SEVEN

The Thirty-Seven-Year Run

How Avoiding One Moment of Pain Cost Me Decades of Living

When the bell rang, I quietly gathered my books and started walking toward my next class, lost in thought. Out of nowhere, my heart began pounding, wild and frantic, like it was trying to break free from my chest. The hallway started closing in around me, narrowing with every step. The voices of other students became muffled and distant, as if I were suddenly underwater. And then I felt it, that terrifying sensation of leaving my own body. I was floating above myself, watching a thirteen-year-old girl have what I didn't yet know was a panic attack.

Three months earlier, I had watched my father collapse and die in our hallway bathroom. Three months of holding in his death. Three months of pretending it hadn't happened. We didn't talk about it. I never cried. And I had no idea where to begin processing the most traumatic event of my young life. That panic attack in the school hallway wasn't random. It was my unhealed grief, finally demanding to be felt. Instead of facing it, I made a decision that would steal the next thirty-seven years of my life. I chose to sweep it under the rug and ignore it instead.

The Body Remembers, Even When We Don't

For nearly four decades, I didn't realize I was living with what Dr. Bessel van der Kolk calls incomplete stress cycles; traumatic experiences frozen in the nervous system because they were never fully processed. His groundbreaking research on

The 37-Year Run

emotional avoidance reveals the devastating cost of unresolved trauma.

When trauma goes unprocessed:

The nervous system stays on high alert, scanning for threats that don't exist.

Avoidant behaviors reinforce neural pathways of fear, making anxiety and panic attacks more likely over time.

The capacity for joy shrinks, because you can't selectively numb emotions. When you avoid pain, you also avoid pleasure.

Physical symptoms emerge as the body tries to express what the mind refuses to acknowledge.

I had unknowingly sentenced myself to a lifetime of emotional prison, all to avoid feeling the devastation of one terrible night when I was twelve years old. Understanding science didn't erase the pain, but it gave me a map. It helped me see that healing wasn't about forgetting, but about finally feeling what I had spent decades running from. Ultimately, finding acceptance.

The Silence of Survival

They weren't just panic attacks; they were invasions, each one dragging me deeper into fear and isolation. Every episode stole a piece of my life, forcing me inward, shrinking my world. I was terrified that someone would see me unravel. So, I withdrew, choosing solitude over the risk of exposure. My greatest fear? Falling apart in public, or worse, in front of a friend.

Gymnastics became my refuge. The structure of routines and the laser focus of competition gave me something solid to hold onto. But outside the gym, I disappeared. In junior high and high school, no one asked me to a school dance. Panic had stolen my voice so completely that people labeled me "shy" and "quiet." I knew I wasn't either. Yet it was easier to wear their labels than to risk them discovering the truth.

I was a girl in survival mode, praying to make it through each day without my nervous system betraying me. The twelve-year-old who found her father dying didn't just lose a parent that night; she lost her trust that love would stay. Her faith in people's loyalty. Her belief that vulnerability was safe. In that moment of unbearable pain, she decided feeling deeply was too dangerous. So, she disappeared emotionally and socially.

The A.V.O.I.D Cycle That Trapped Me

Through the years of working with clients and reflecting on my own patterns, I identified what I call the A.V.O.I.D Cycle- A five-step framework that explains how emotional avoidance keeps us stuck.

A - ACTIVATE the Escape Response- When painful emotions arise, immediately look for an exit; distractions, busyness, relationships, anything to avoid sitting with the feeling.

V - VALIDATE the Avoidance- Tell yourself stories that make avoidance seem wise: "I'm being strong," "It's better not to dwell," "I need to move on," "Crying won't bring him back."

O - ORGANIZE Your Life Around the Avoidance- Structure your entire existence to prevent triggering the avoided emotion. Avoid certain places, people, conversations, or activities that may trigger painful feelings.

I - ISOLATE from Support- Push away people who might encourage you to process what you're avoiding, surrounding yourself only with those who enable your emotional numbness.

D - DEEPEN the Pattern- Each successful avoidance reinforces the cycle, making you more likely to avoid the next difficult emotion, until avoidance becomes your default response to all pain.

The 37-Year Run

The Wound Beneath the Silence

The most devastating consequence of my emotional avoidance came just before high school graduation. My silence and invisibility didn't protect me; they made me prey. Predators can spot someone who won't fight back.

My high school story was supposed to end with graduation. Instead, it ended with rape. And what did I do with that trauma? Exactly what I had done with my father's death: I swept it under the rug. I blamed myself. I told myself I shouldn't have gone to that party. I convinced myself it was my fault. The hardest part to process, even now, is that I didn't call it rape until I was in my late forties. It wasn't until I began my healing journey, slowing down enough to feel, to process, and to name what happened. It was then that I could finally say the word: rape.

I learned that you can't heal what you can't feel. You can't transform what you won't acknowledge. By living invisibly, by never accessing my voice, by existing in constant survival mode I had made myself vulnerable to someone who saw my silence as an opportunity. The emotional avoidance that began with losing my father had weakened my ability to set boundaries and protect myself.

There's something important to know about trauma: it has a way of building on itself. Each unprocessed wound doesn't just sit quietly in isolation; it creates a blueprint for how we handle the next violation. My father's death taught me that pain was too dangerous to feel, so I buried it. That burial became my survival strategy. And when you're a young woman who has already practiced disappearing for six years, who has no access to her voice, who believes that staying silent keeps you safe. You become a perfect target for predators who can sense silence from across a room.

What happened to me wasn't random chance; it was the result of wounds I didn't know how to heal colliding with someone willing to exploit them. The twelve-year-old who couldn't process her father's death became the eighteen-year-old who couldn't name her rape. Years of sweeping trauma under the rug didn't erase my pain; it exposed my vulnerability. And for decades, I kept repeating the pattern, each new hurt stacking on top of the old ones, building a mountain of unprocessed grief I carried everywhere, convinced that feeling nothing was safer than feeling everything.

Here's what I now understand: unfelt pain doesn't disappear. It metastasizes. It spreads through your life, poisoning your relationships, stealing your voice, and keeping you trapped in patterns that destroy you slowly from the inside out.

Avoidance Isn't Safety

The panic attacks were just a symptom. The real poison was the pattern I created the day my father died. When something hurts too much to handle, sweep it under the rug and pretend it never happened. For thirty-seven years, I was consistent in avoiding anything that required me to feel pain, process loss, or face uncomfortable truths. A man would cheat on me, and instead of confronting the betrayal, I'd say, "Where do you want to go to dinner?" "Let's plan a vacation."

My nervous system couldn't handle the confrontation, so I defaulted to distraction. When someone treated me poorly, I'd shrink into politeness, smiling, changing the subject, all while working hard to keep the peace. Relationships would end badly, and instead of processing what went wrong, I'd isolate myself for months, sometimes years, before I could face the pain of dating again. Everything painful went under the rug. Every difficult conversation was avoided.

The 37-Year Run

My body didn't know how to process pain. Instead, my nervous system would flip into fight, flight, or freeze mode. Avoiding the present problem felt easier than dealing with a dysregulated nervous system. Every moment that required emotional courage was met with emotional retreat. I became consistently inconsistent with my own healing. And that pattern cost me everything.

Swept Under the Rug: How Avoiding Grief Made Me a Stranger to Myself

For thirty-seven years, I avoided the grief of my father's death. I didn't just suppress the pain; I built my entire emotional survival system around it. My nervous system learned to disconnect from vulnerability, silence my truth, and numb the ache. What I didn't realize was that this blueprint didn't just shape how I handled loss; it quietly dictated every relationship, every reaction, and every retreat from healing. The cost wasn't just emotional. It was a life that lived with fear of feeling.

My pattern became simple: deny, avoid, and sweep it under the rug. I let people walk all over me, not because I didn't know better, but because keeping the peace felt safer than facing the storm inside. I trained myself not to feel anything too deeply. Betrayal? Ignore it. Pain? Bury it. Disrespect? Tolerate it. Because to feel would mean opening the floodgates to a grief I'd been running from since I was twelve.

That twelve-year-old girl believed her father had abandoned her. The facts in her mind were: he died and left us with zero financial security. My mother had to leave being a stay-at-home mom to find work to provide for us. "My loss wasn't just a parent, it was the collapse of safety, stability, and the illusion that life plays fair. I never processed that loss; I formed a core wound of abandonment that shaped every relationship that followed.

Valerie Maksym

In a way that feels almost cruel, I learned to crave any attention, even the kind that hurt, because at least it meant I wasn't invisible. I built my life around survival, not truth. I became a machine, programmed to mimic connection without ever tasting it. Friendships, love, they were motions I mastered, not moments I lived. I was there, but never whole. Present, but hollow.

The way I avoided processing my father's death became the way I avoided everything, including truly living. My father's death shattered something fundamental in me, and instead of examining the pieces, I buried them. In doing so, I didn't just avoid grief, I avoided myself. I turned away from my feelings, my truth, my needs, and my voice. That moment became the blueprint for how I would navigate the emotional terrain of my life: suppress, silence, survive. Every time I swept grief under the rug, I was also sweeping away pieces of my identity, my desires, and my chance to heal. By not processing his absence, I unknowingly denied myself the ability to be fully present in my own life. I wasn't just grieving a loss; I was grieving the life I never allowed myself too fully live.

Dr. Gabor Maté's research shows that chronic emotional suppression leads to a 400% increase in chronic illness, higher rates of anxiety and depression, impaired ability to form authentic relationships, and a haunting sense of "living someone else's life." That was me. Living someone else's life. A life built on silence, survival, and self-abandonment. But here's the truth: healing begins the moment you stop sweeping it under the rug and start feeling. The moment you stop being the doormat and begin being the doorway to your truth, your pain, and your power.

If you're reading this and recognizing your own patterns, know this: you are not broken. You are buried. And everything you've swept under the rug is waiting, not to haunt you, but to heal you. You don't have to live as a stranger to yourself anymore. You can come home. One feeling at a time.

The Cemetery That Finally Broke Me Open

The breaking point didn't happen in a therapist's office. It showed up on a rainy afternoon when I was fifty, driving away from a bodybuilding competition photoshoot. Out of nowhere, a quiet whisper surfaced inside me: Stop by your father's grave. I tried to ignore it, just like I had for thirty-seven years. But as I got closer to the cemetery where he was buried, the whisper turned into a roar I couldn't silence. So, I pulled in, and the moment my tires touched the cemetery grounds, tears began pouring uncontrollably down my face. Between the rain on my windshield and the flood in my eyes, I could barely see the road.

I thought I knew where his grave was, but after wandering for what felt like forever, I realized I was lost. I had two choices: leave and continue the pattern of avoidance that had ruled my life, or swallow my pride and call my mother for help. My ego screamed No! I didn't want her to know I was there, didn't want her to witness the unraveling I'd kept buried for decades. Something stronger than pride took over, and I dialed her number. She guided me through the cemetery over the phone until I stood before the headstone: Thomas Jay Maksym.

I stood there in the rain, an umbrella in my hand, talking to my father for the first time since I was twelve. And I cried harder than I'd ever cried in my life. For a full hour, I let thirty-seven years of grief pour out of me. "I'm sorry I never cried for you," I whispered. "I'm sorry I pretended your death didn't destroy me. I'm sorry I spent my whole life running from the pain of losing you." In that hour, I didn't just mourn his passing; I mourned the version of myself I had abandoned in order to survive. I felt something shift; something was released. It felt as if the rain wasn't just falling around me; it was cleansing me from the inside, washing decades of silence, denial, and emotional exile away.

The C.O.U.R.A.G.E. Protocol: Facing What I Spent a Lifetime Avoiding

That moment in the cemetery became more than just a confrontation with grief. It became the template for how I would finally begin to face everything I had spent decades avoiding. I call it the C.O.U.R.A.G.E Protocol, because it takes real courage to feel what you've been running from.

C – Commit to Feeling
I made a conscious decision to stop running. No more numbing, no more pretending. I chose to feel, even when the emotions felt too big, too messy, too overwhelming.

O – Open to the Pain
Instead of shutting down, I opened up. I gave myself permission to sit with the pain I had buried for years. I carved out space to let the emotions move through me, without judgment or resistance.

U – Understand the Message
I began asking myself: What is this emotion trying to tell me? Pain isn't just suffering; it's information. It reveals what I need, what I've lost, and what I must change.

R – Release Through Expression
I found ways to let it out. I cried. I journaled. I talked to people who felt safe to share my feelings with. I revisited places that held meaning. I moved my body. I allowed the emotions to flow through me instead of staying trapped inside.

A – Acknowledge the Courage
I reminded myself that feeling pain isn't weakness, it's strength. It takes far more bravery to face your wounds than to ignore them. I honored that courage every step of the way.

The 37-Year Run

G – Give Yourself Time

Healing didn't happen in a single moment. It came in layers, waves, and seasons. I learned to be patient with myself, to let the process unfold without rushing or forcing it.

E – Emerge Transformed

And slowly, I began to change and transform. As I processed the pain, I rediscovered joy, connection, and authenticity. I wasn't just healing the hurt; I was reclaiming my life. I stopped living in avoidance and started living in truth.

The Voice That Returned

Within months of processing my father's death, something unexpected and miraculous happened: I found my voice. Not just the ability to speak, but the ability to know what I thought, what I felt, what I wanted, and what I would no longer accept. The panic attacks that had gripped me for decades began to loosen their hold. The doormat I had become, the one who tolerated anything to keep the peace, started to disappear. I stopped asking a cheater what he wanted for dinner. I started saying things I never imagined I could: "That's not acceptable to me." "I need time to process this." "I'm hurt by what you said." "I disagree with you." "This ends now." Finding my voice didn't happen in one defining moment. It was something I had to choose every single day; a practice of speaking up, even when it felt uncomfortable, until it became part of who I am.

Learning to feel instead of fleeing required a kind of consistency I had never practiced before; the courage to stay when every instinct screamed to run. It meant choosing to feel rather than numb. Truth over denial. Processing over pretending. And with every choice, my voice grew stronger. It wasn't just about speaking; it was about reclaiming the part of me that had been silenced for so long. The part that knew what I deserved. The part that could finally say, I matter.

The Moment That's Waiting

Your unprocessed loss. Your buried trauma. Your silenced voice. Your abandoned dreams. They're waiting for you. Waiting to be felt, acknowledged, and finally integrated. The younger version of you, the one who experienced something too overwhelming to handle, is still there, quietly hoping you'll turn around and witness their pain. Your younger self doesn't need you to fix the past. They need you to say: *"You mattered, you deserved compassion, not abandonment."* Stop running from the part of yourself that's been calling for your attention for years. Turn toward them with the tenderness you'd offer to a frightened child.

Stop being consistent in your avoidance. Start being consistent with your courage. The healing that unlocks every other area of your life is just one honest conversation away; the one you've been postponing with yourself. Your transformed life could be waiting on the other side of the pain you've been avoiding. The emotions you've been running from may hold the keys to the freedom you've been seeking. Stop running. Allow yourself to feel. Begin your healing journey. Start living.

You don't have to do this alone. Professional support can guide you and ensure safety as you walk this path. But the invitation remains: Your healing begins the moment you're ready to face what you've been avoiding.

CHAPTER EIGHT

The Fierce Love That Left Scars

How I Learned to Build Instead of Destroy the Relationships That Mattered Most

"Why a butterfly with the word Patience underneath it?" The tattoo artist asked as the needle buzzed against my skin. The sharp sting was nothing compared to the pain that had led me to his chair. "Because I'm a wrecking ball," I said, the words tumbling out before I could stop them. I've wrecked more than I care to admit by rushing ahead instead of slowing down. When I pause, I see what is real. When I don't, I bulldoze through things I barely understand. The butterfly symbolized my desire to transform rather than destroy. And the word patience? It was a desperate attempt to tattoo a reminder onto my body, because I couldn't trust my mind to remember what my impatience had already cost me.

As the ink etched into my skin, my chest tightened with the realization: I was literally carving my failures into my flesh. Not out of self-punishment, but out of a need to never forget the impulsive decisions that have hurt the people I love most; my children. What did it cost me? Only the most important relationships in the world. After months of laying down everyone else's baggage, learning to show up authentically, managing triggers, breaking free from mental prisons, tearing down emotional walls, and finally letting go of what no longer served me, I thought I had mastered the art of healing. I was making better choices. I was setting boundaries. I was building genuine connections. But this tattoo wasn't just body art. It was a mothers' vow, a permanent reminder to stop wreaking havoc on her children's lives with her own unhealed trauma. It was the mark of someone who had finally decided to transform, not perform.

Breaking the Cycle: Parenting Through the Fog of Trauma

When I was raising my kids, I didn't realize I was stuck in a cycle, repeating the same patterns I had learned in my own childhood. I wasn't doing it on purpose. I was trying to do better, trying to fix what had hurt me. But instead, I ended up passing down the very pain I was trying to escape. It was like handing my children a toxic inheritance I never meant to give.

Parents who've experienced trauma often react impulsively not because they don't love their children, but because their bodies and minds are still stuck in survival mode. Everyday problems feel like emergencies. Small disagreements feel like threats. And the instinct to protect turns into a need to control.

According to trauma expert Dr. Gabor Maté, unresolved childhood trauma can lead to reactive parenting. The brain interprets normal stressors as threats, and the fear center takes over. Rational thinking shuts down; stress hormones flood the system, and decisions are made to relieve immediate discomfort, often at the cost of long-term emotional safety for the child.

I had been parenting from that place for years, making choices that soothed my own anxiety but shattered my children's sense of security. Every decision felt like life or death to me, but I didn't realize I was creating that same terror for them. I wasn't a bad mother. I was a mother in pain. But pain, when left unhealed, doesn't just stay inside; it spills out, shaping the lives of those we love most.

The 37-Year Run

Reflection Prompt

Take a moment to reflect on your own upbringing and how it may be influencing your parenting or relationships today. Ask yourself:

What patterns do I notice repeating from my childhood?

When I feel triggered, what do I tend to do: shut down, or lash out?

What would it look like to respond from a place of calm instead of urgency?

Write down one moment where you reacted impulsively and one where you responded with intention. What was the difference in outcome?

Action Step

Choose one small moment this week to pause before reacting. When you feel triggered, take a breath and ask yourself: "Is this an emergency, or is this a moment to slow down and choose differently?" That pause is where healing begins.

The Night That Built My Armor

The pattern that nearly destroyed my family began on a night that still haunts my dreams. I was thirteen years old, just months after my father had died, when I heard my mother's terrified voice echoing down the hallway. I crept to my bedroom door and peeked out to see my stepfather a man we barely knew, holding a shotgun to her head. The metal gleamed cold in the dim light as her body shook with sobs that came from somewhere deeper than her lungs.

My bare feet hit the cold floor as I climbed out of my bedroom window, heart pounding so hard I thought it might burst. I ran to the neighbors for help, propelled by pure terror. But at that moment, something inside me shifted. I made a decision that would shape the next three decades of my life.

I would never be that powerless again.

I would never wait for someone else to protect me. I would take control, move fast, and dominate every situation before it could dominate me. The thirteen-year-old girl who had just lost her father, and nearly lost her mother, decided that patience was dangerous, vulnerability was deadly, and slowing down gave others the chance to hurt you. I believed it was safer to be the one doing the wrecking than the one getting wrecked.

The Cycle I Didn't Know I Was Repeating

By the time I had children of my own, I had perfected the art of bulldozing through life. Every decision felt urgent. Every relationship shift felt like survival. Every moment of discomfort felt like an emergency that demanded immediate action. The most devastating realization came years later. When I saw the exact pattern, I had sworn I'd never repeat unfolding in my own parenting. Just months after my father died, my mother came home married to a man my brother and I barely knew. She was twenty-nine, overwhelmed, and likely terrified of raising two children alone. In her desperation, she rushed into a marriage that nearly killed her. She brought danger into our home because she didn't slow down long enough to truly know who she was inviting into our lives.

And thirty years later, I found myself doing the same thing. I rushed my children through my divorce and straight into a second marriage, never pausing to process their feelings about the stranger I was asking them to accept as their stepfather. I was so afraid of the loneliness I felt; I dragged them through my chaos without ever asking what it felt like to be them.

The 37-Year Run

The conversation that would eventually change everything was still years away. But the damage was already being done, one impulsive decision at a time.

Reflection Prompt: What Are You Carrying Forward?

Take a moment to reflect on your own family history. Ask yourself:

What patterns from my childhood do I see showing up in my parenting or relationships?

Have I ever made a decision out of fear or urgency that affected someone I love?

The F.O.C.U.S. Method: From Reactivity to Intentional Connection

After finally recognizing my wrecking ball pattern and seeing myself clearly in the wreckage I'd created, I knew I needed a system in place that would help me to make better decisions. A system that builds strong connections and relationships. That's when I developed the F.O.C.U.S. Method, a framework for slowing down, tuning in, and choosing connection over chaos.

F – FREEZE Before Acting
When that familiar urgency rises, the need to fix, decide, or escape, take a moment and freeze. Pause, then count to ten. Take three deep breaths. Ask yourself: "Am I running toward something healthy, or away from something uncomfortable?" I learned to recognize that uneasy feeling in my gut as a signal: I was about to make a critical decision from a place of fear, not love.

O – OBSERVE the Ripple Effects
Before making any decisions, consider how it will affect everyone in your family system. Ask: "How will this decision impact the people I love most?" I started visualizing my choices

like stones thrown into a pond. I had to see all the ripples before I let one drop.

C – CONSULT Your People

Include those who will be affected by your decisions, especially your children, in age-appropriate ways. Ask: "How do you feel about this possibility?" Then listen. Listen to what your kids are saying as well as what they are not saying. Without defending, explaining, or minimizing their concerns. Their truth matters.

U – UNDERSTAND the Real Timeline

Most decisions that feel urgent aren't. Take time to understand all aspects of your decisions. Ask yourself: What happens if I wait 30 days? Six months? Or a year? The world rarely ends when we take time to think. Slowing down creates space for clarity.

S – SLOW DOWN to Speed Up

Thoughtful decisions save time in the long run. Slow down, pause, and reflect on all scenarios before making your decision. When you slow down, you lower the chances of needing to redo, repair, or apologize later. Going slow isn't a weakness; it's wisdom.

The Zoom Call That Broke Me Open

The breaking point came about a year after my second divorce. Guilt was eating me alive, sleepless nights spent replaying every rushed decision, every moment I had chosen fear over my children's stability. I knew I needed to hear their truth, even if it shattered me. At the time, I was launching my life coaching business and asked each of my children if they'd be willing to do a few coaching-style Zoom calls with me. They said yes. I had the privilege of having my kids as my first clients. Those moments were priceless, and I'll never forget them.

The 37-Year Run

I scheduled individual video calls with each of my four children, wearing my professional coaching hat and doing my best to create a safe space for them to share openly. I had my questions prepared, and my framework was ready. I thought I was prepared for anything. I wasn't prepared for what my twenty-three-year-old son would say. His face filled the screen, but his eyes looked distant, as if he were seeing something far beyond the walls of my living room. When I asked how my choices had affected him, his voice came out flat, emotionless, like he'd rehearsed the words in his head for years. "Mom, I saw two options for my life: prison or death." The words hit me like a physical blow. My coaching composure crumbled instantly. The framework I'd been trained in, staying neutral, asking open-ended questions, holding space without judgment, felt impossible when the person on the other side of the screen was my child, telling me he had once contemplated ending his life because of the chaos I had brought into our home.

I sat there, staring at his face, unable to catch my breath. This is my baby. The little boy who used to climb into my bed during thunderstorms. The teenager who once trusted me with his dreams. And in that moment, I realized I hadn't just failed as a mother, I had been so busy trying to find love for myself that I had created a war zone for my children to survive through.

Rebuilding After the Rupture

That Zoom call didn't just break me; it opened me. It forced me to stop hiding behind good intentions and finally face the impact of my actions. I couldn't undo the past, but I could choose how I showed up moving forward. Repair doesn't begin with perfection. It starts with presence. With the willingness to sit in the discomfort of what's been broken and say, "I'm here now. I'm listening. I will do better." The more I listened to my kids, without interruption, the more I learned from them. Every conversation became a lesson in patience, perspective, and presence. They taught me that wisdom isn't born only from years lived; it blooms when you lean in, hear the spoken as well as the unspoken, and let it change you.

Reflection Prompt: Facing the Impact

Take a moment to reflect on a time when someone you love tried to tell you how your actions affected them. Ask yourself:

Did I truly listen, or did I defend myself?

Was I more focused on being right than being present?

What would it look like to revisit that moment with humility and curiosity?

Write a letter (even if you never send it) to someone you may have hurt unintentionally. Focus not on explaining yourself, but on acknowledging their experience.

Healing Action Step: Start the Repair

Choose one person you've hurt, whether recently or long ago, and reach out to them. You don't need a perfect script. You need honesty. You could say something like: "I've been thinking about how my actions may have affected you. I'm not reaching out to defend myself. I am reaching out because I truly want to understand and take responsibility for what I unknowingly may have done. If you're open to it, I'd love to hear your truth." Even if they're not ready to talk, your willingness to own your impact is a powerful step toward healing, for them and for you.

The W.E.A.T.H.E.R. System: How Parents Shape Emotional Climate

That devastating conversation with my son, and the work I've done with clients, led me to identify what I now call the W.E.A.T.H.E.R. System: a framework for understanding how parental choices can shape the emotional climate children must navigate.

W – Words Matter More Than Intent

What you say to children becomes their inner voice. Saying, "Your dad and I are splitting up. You'll be fine," creates a storm. Saying, "I know this is hard. How are you feeling about the changes happening in our family?" invites calm. Words don't just inform; they form a child's sense of safety.

A few other examples of Storm sentences versus Calm statements:

Storm: "We're moving next week. Don't worry about it."

Calm: "We're planning to move soon. What questions do you have about the new place?"

Storm: "We're having another baby. Deal with it."

Calm: "We're excited about a new baby joining the family. How do you feel about becoming an older sibling?"

Storm: "We're broke. Stop asking for things."

Calm: "Money is tight right now, but we'll figure it out together. What's most important to you?"

Storm: "Why can't you be more like your sibling?"

Calm: "You're both unique and special. What do you love most about yourself?"

E – Emotions Set the Temperature

Your emotional state becomes the family thermostat. It sets the climate for connection or disconnection. My desperation to avoid being alone created a storm system of instability and hypervigilance. My children learned to read my emotional weather like meteorologists, scanning for signs of danger before they could relax. When I was anxious, the air was heavy. When I was frustrated, the atmosphere crackled. When I was calm, they could finally breathe. Children don't just hear your words; they feel your emotional temperature. They absorb it. They adapt to it. And over time, they learn to regulate themselves based on the forecast you create.

A – Actions Create the Forecast
Children may be able to predict their future safety based on your past behavior. My history of rushing into relationships and the dramatic endings that followed taught my kids that chaos was just around the corner. They lived in constant preparation for the next emotional hurricane.

Actions don't just tell a story; they set the stage. The choices you make become a part of the forecast your children learn to trust or fear. Consistency creates calm. Instability creates storms. When your actions align with safety, children can finally exhale.

T – Timing Affects Everything
Timing can either soothe or shock. Rushing major decisions creates emotional whiplash. Taking time creates calm, predictable seasons that allow children to adjust, trust, and feel secure. What felt urgent to me felt unsafe to them. Stability isn't just about what you choose; it's about when you choose it.

H – Healing Changes the Climate
When a parent addresses their own trauma, the atmosphere shifts from survival mode to growth mode. My healing journey didn't just change me; it also allowed my adult children to begin their own healing journey. When we model what it looks like to face pain and choose restoration, we create a climate where safety and hope can thrive. Healing isn't just personal; it's generational.

E – Empathy Provides Shelter
Children need more than solutions; they need to feel seen, heard, and understood. When we dismiss, minimize, or rush their emotions, we leave them exposed to the storm. Empathy

is the roof that shields them from emotional downpour, and listening is the foundation that keeps them steady.

What Empathy Does:

Creates an emotional shelter where healing becomes possible.

Builds trust and resilience over time.

Offers safety without judgment or pressure.

How to Practice It:

Pause before responding; validation often matters more than fixing.

Use phrases like "I hear you" or "That sounds really hard" to hold space.

Remember: Empathy doesn't mean solving feelings; it means staying present with them.

When children feel sheltered by empathy, they learn that their emotions are valid and that they are never alone in the storm.

R – Repair Makes Renewal Possible
Acknowledging the mistake and committing to consistent change can transform even the most damaged relationships. Repair isn't just saying "I'm sorry," it's taking it a step further and proving change through daily actions that rebuild trust.

What Repair Does:

Opens the door for healing and reconnection.

Shows accountability and respect for the relationship.

Creates space for growth and renewal.

How to Practice It:

Acknowledge the harm clearly; avoid excuses.

Commit to specific changes and follow through consistently.

Demonstrate repair through actions, not just words.

Repair is a process, not a moment. When we pair honest acknowledgment with sustained effort, broken bonds can become stronger than before.

The Emotional Battlefield I Didn't See

What followed was a devastating moment in my life. My son painted a vivid picture of what it was like to grow up caught in the crossfire, between his mother's desperate search for love and a stepfather who saw him as an obstacle. "You were always trying to keep the peace," he said, his voice heavy with years of accumulated hurt. I could see the little boy he used to be in his eyes, confused, scared, trying to understand why his mother kept shrinking. "If you took his side, we felt abandoned. If you took our side, he punished you, and we watched you disappear even more." My throat tightened as memories flooded back with sickening clarity. I had spent those years as a mediator, trying to manage everyone's emotions, exhausting myself in the process. And while I thought I was protecting my children, I was teaching them that love meant disappearing. "We turned to drugs to numb the pain," my son continued, each word landing like a blow to my chest. "The chaos you brought into our home was so unbearable that self-medicating felt like the only way to survive."

I wanted to defend myself. To explain my intentions. To justify my choices. But I could see in his face what those explanations had already cost him. This was my handsome boy, the one who used to climb into my bed during thunderstorms, the teenager who once trusted me with his dreams. And instead of thinking about college or his future, he had been calculating whether prison or death offered better odds than surviving the wreckage of my decisions.

The 37-Year Run

From Wreckage to Repair: Rebuilding Trust One Conversation at a Time

After that Zoom call, I didn't try to fix everything overnight. I didn't rush to make grand gestures or offer long-winded explanations. I did something far more difficult: I paused, gave myself space, and sat with the discomfort. I embraced the silence and stayed grounded in the truth.

Rebuilding trust with my children wasn't about convincing them I had changed; it was about showing them, consistently, through small, daily choices. It was about listening more than speaking. It was about asking questions without needing to control the answers. It was about letting them feel angry, hurt, and sad, without rushing them through those emotions. I began to say things I had never said before like, "I understand why you're angry. You have every right to be." "I'm not here to defend myself. I want to understand your experience." "I'm committed to doing better, even if it takes time for you to believe that." Gradually, things began to change. It wasn't perfect, and it didn't happen all at once, but the walls started to crack, letting the first rays of light slip through.

What Broke Between Us

I sat in complete silence for what felt like an eternity. Maybe, for the first time in his life, I was fully present, sitting with his pain. Here was my son, now an adult but still my child, so broken by the chaos I'd created that he'd chosen a slow-motion suicide through the streets. Not a note or a plan, but a life so dangerous that death or prison were the only destinations. He wasn't trying to die; he just wasn't trying to live. The silence stretched between us through the computer screen. I could hear my own heartbeat. Tears started burning hot tracks down my cheeks. This was the cost of my impatience. This was the price of my fear. This is what can happen when a mother chooses her

comfort over her child's needs and safety.
The apology that came out of me felt hollow considering the magnitude of what I'd unconsciously put him through. How do you apologize for creating such a toxic environment that your child chooses numbness over feeling, despair over hope? Regardless, I still apologized. "I'm sorry for everything I put you through," I said, my voice breaking on every word. Inside, I said to myself, I repeated the same thing I experienced when my father died. My mom came home married to a stranger, and I swore I'd never do that to my kids. But I managed to do it anyway. Oh, how I wish I could have handled things differently. He received my apology and nodded. His simple acknowledgment broke something open in my heart.

A Promise Made in Truth

"From this day forward," I told him, "I will make better decisions. I will include you and your siblings in any important decision-making that affects you all. Your opinions will matter. "Through the screen, I saw skepticism in his eyes. He'd heard promises before. I've said things would be different before. The little boy who once watched me disappear into unhealthy relationships had grown into a man who'd learned not to trust his mother's words. Why should he believe me now? Because this time felt different, I finally understood the actual cost of my impatience. It wasn't only about my happiness anymore; it was about their survival and healing. It was no longer about my fear of being alone; it was about their right to feel safe in their own home.

Healing in Real Time

When I began dating John, I did something new. I included my children in my dating life once I knew we were exclusive. Instead of announcing my decisions, I asked for their input. "How do you feel about me dating John?" "How would you feel if I were to marry him?" "Do you see any red flags?" The transformation was gradual, but undeniable. My children watched me as I took the time to listen to their input, rather than dismissing them like I had in the past. They sensed the change in our relationship when I chose to focus on building a healthy emotional connection with the man I hoped to marry, rather than letting my fear of being alone take the lead. They saw me practice the F.O.C.U.S. method in real time, slowing down enough to consider how my choices would ripple through their lives, too.

Before John proposed, he asked for my son's blessing, the same son who once believed his future held only prison or death. At our wedding, that son walked me down the aisle, not with resentment, but with pride. His smile as he placed my hand in John's wasn't forced; it radiated genuine joy for a mother who had finally chosen healing over hiding.

When Healing Became Contagious

Today, my son has built everything he feels he lacked as a child: stability, emotional safety, and a sense of predictable love. Despite his father's abandonment, despite years of chaos and instability, despite the pain that once made him consider prison or death as his only options, he has become an incredible husband and father. He broke the cycle. He chose healing over perpetuating pain. And what I'm about to share still brings tears to my eyes. When I began my healing journey, my children, without me saying a word, began their own. My commitment to getting healthy permitted them to heal as well. They saw that change was possible, and patterns could be broken. That love could mean safety instead of chaos.

When Parents Choose Growth

Dr. Dan Siegel's research on family healing reveals a powerful truth: when parents take genuine accountability for emotionally unsafe behavior, children's stress hormones can decrease by up to 60% within six months. But here's the key, accountability isn't just about saying "I'm sorry." It's about consistently changing behavior over time.

Children of parents who practice true repair show:

Improved emotional regulation

Higher self-esteem

Better relationship skills as adults

Reduced rates of depression and anxiety

The power isn't in being a perfect parent. It's in being a parent who is brave enough to face their mistakes and committed enough to do better. I didn't know of this research when I first began my healing journey, but I saw it unfold in real time. As I took accountability and made changes in my life, I watched my children begin to breathe easier, trust more deeply, and heal.

The Wrecking Ball Assessment

Ask yourself these questions:

Have you made major life decisions without considering how they'd affect your children?

Do your children walk on eggshells around you?

Have you prioritized your need for a relationship over their need for stability?

Do your children feel safe sharing their real problems and feelings with you?

Have you ever asked them directly how your choices have affected them?

If you answered yes to three or more, it might be time for your own kitchen table conversation. Your children could be waiting for you to be brave enough to ask the hard questions and strong enough to hear their honest answers.

The 4-Step Family Repair Process

These steps are drawn from both personal experience and research on family healing. They're not about perfection; they're about presence, accountability, and transformation.

Step 1: Own Your Choices

Before healing can begin, you have to face the truth. Not the polished version. Not the "I did my best" narrative. The real truth. Take a hard look at the choices you made and how they shaped your children's lives. Name them. Own them. No excuses. No justifications. Your kids don't need perfection; they need honesty. They need to know you see the impact clearly and that you're willing to take responsibility. That's where trust begins. That's where repair starts.

Step 2: Hear Them Fully

Listening isn't passive; it's an act of courage. When your children speak their truth, let it land. Don't interrupt. Don't defend. Don't rush to explain what you meant or why you did what you did. Their truth is their truth. Honor it. Healing can't happen if you argue with their pain or minimize their experience. This is their moment to be heard; entirely, freely, without fear of being dismissed. Your job is simple, but not easy: stay present, stay quiet, and let their words matter.

Step 3: Commit With Clarity

Promises without substance break trust. Vague intentions sound good, but don't heal wounds. If you're going to make a commitment, make it concrete, specific, measurable, and visible. Instead of saying, "I'll do better," say, "I will ask for your input before making any decision that affects our family." Give them something solid to hold on to; something they can see, feel, and trust. Real change is built on clear commitments, not empty words.

Step 4: Let Your Actions Speak

Words matter, but they're not enough. Promises don't rebuild trust; it's rebuilt by patterns. Show them this time is different. Every day is an opportunity to prove your commitment. Small, consistent actions speak louder than any apology. Be present. Be accountable. Be steady. I didn't learn this from a textbook; I lived it. And as I practiced it, I watched my children begin to heal. Not because I was perfect, but because I showed up consistently, willing to put in the work.

The Conversation That Changed Everything

The table where I asked my children for forgiveness became the birthplace of our happy, loving, committed family; not the one built on my fear of being alone, but the one built on honesty, repair, and the radical belief that children's feelings matter as much as adults' fears.

My children never doubted my love. But they doubted my ability to keep them emotionally safe, and they were right to. I had shown them, time and again, that my comfort mattered more than their stability. That my fear mattered more than their security.

The hardest conversation I ever had as a mother turned out to be the most important one. Because silence about parental mistakes doesn't protect children from their impact. It only teaches them that their pain doesn't matter.

The Forecast for Healing

Every choice you make sends ripples through your family. For years, I created waves of chaos, and my children were the ones struggling to stay afloat. But when I chose patience and real repair, the ripples shifted. Chaos gave way to calm. Hurt gave way to healing. That healing became our family's new legacy.

Your choices shape the emotional climate in your home. Your kids don't need perfection; they need honesty about your imperfections and a commitment to change.

I no longer need ink on my foot to remind me to slow down. The memory of my son's words, "prison or death," is a reminder enough. The son who once saw only two dark options now sees infinite possibilities, for himself and for us. That's the power of a parent who finally chose healing over hiding, patience over panic, and their children's safety over their own fear of being alone.

Stop being the storm that wrecks what you love most. Start being the safe harbor where they can rest. Your children are waiting for you to create sunshine instead of chaos, stability instead of drama, and patience instead of panic. The forecast for your family's future? It's in your hands.

CHAPTER NINE

The Space Between Letting Go and Finding Love
Why Letting Go Can Feel Like Dying

One morning, I awoke to an unrecognizable feeling: pure joy, profound peace, and a sense of freedom so surreal it seemed like a dream. For the first time, I wasn't carrying the weight of everyone else's expectations, pain, or chaos. I was fully in my own lane, holding only what was mine to carry. The compulsion to pick up other people's baggage had vanished. That moment is etched in my memory; I felt a shift so profound that I felt light, unburdened, and ready to embrace everything I had ever dreamed of doing, seeing, and becoming.

The real test came shortly after, when someone I care about was going through an unusually difficult time in their life. Without even realizing it, I went back to my programmed way, and I picked up their emotional baggage and absorbed their pain so deeply that I felt paralyzed. I didn't want to go anywhere or do anything. I couldn't see a solution, and the weight of their suffering became mine. This familiar pattern of taking on others' life challenges is one I had repeated for years. But this time, something shifted. I caught myself in the act of carrying their heavy load and reminded myself that their battles are not mine to carry. I gently set their bag down, not out of indifference, but out of love. I reminded myself that I am here to support, to walk beside them, to pray for them, but not to lose myself in their pain. I needed to stay strong, not just for me, but for them. Strength emerges when you stand with compassion, clarity, and resilience, not when you lose yourself in their pain.

That moment reinforced everything I had been learning. Real progress had begun to show up in every corner of my life. I was present. I was connected. I was me, not a mirror of someone else, not a shadow fading into the background. I had learned to face and heal the triggers that once held me hostage. By doing so, I broke free from the mental prison I had unknowingly built. For the first time, I wasn't just surviving; I was thriving and feeling good about life. This feeling didn't fade with morning coffee. I had earned this joy through every painful step of healing, and now it was mine to keep.

The Terror of Letting Go

A client's story completely shifted my understanding of why we hold on to what hurts us. Shelly had been divorced for two years. And yet, every morning, she still checked her ex-husband's LinkedIn profile while sipping her coffee. She still drove past their old house on weekends. She still wore her wedding ring, now on her right hand, "because it felt weird without it." "I know I should let go," she said, tears streaming down her cheeks during our video call. "Everyone tells me to let him go. I tell myself to move on every single day. So why can't I let go?"

As I watched this brilliant, successful woman torture herself with digital breadcrumbs from a marriage that had long ended, something clicked. Shelly wasn't broken. She wasn't weak. She was experiencing something called the neurobiological terror of letting go.

The shift began with one realization: your brain is wired for survival, just as it was thousands of years ago. When someone important leaves our life, whether through death, divorce, or emotional distance, your nervous system reacts as if the ground beneath you has vanished. It doesn't separate emotional loss from physical danger; both ignite the same primal alarm: "Warning! This threatens survival! Hold on, don't let go!"

Shelly's daily LinkedIn visits weren't pathetic; they were her ancient survival instincts scanning the horizon for signs of belonging. Her body believed that staying connected even through pain was safer than stepping into the terrifying unknown of letting go.

Dr. Joe Dispenza's research reveals: "When you think the same thoughts, make the same choices, demonstrate the same behaviors, and create the same experiences, you will produce the same emotions every day. And those emotions drive the same thoughts."

Shelly was stuck in what researchers call a cognitive emotional loop. Her thoughts about her ex triggered familiar emotions, sadness, hope, and anger. Those emotions drove behaviors like checking social media and driving by the house. Those behaviors created experiences that reinforced the same thoughts. And the loop continued, keeping her emotionally tethered to a past that no longer existed.

Breaking the Loop

Once I understood the loop Shelly was trapped in, I knew that healing wouldn't come from forcing her to "move on." It had to come from interrupting the cycle, gently, consistently, and with compassion. Here's the strategy we used, one that can help anyone stuck in a loop of emotional repetition:

Step 1: Awareness Without Judgment

The first step is noticing the loop in real time. Not with shame. Not with self-criticism. Just awareness. "I'm checking his LinkedIn again." "I'm driving by the house again." "I'm replaying the same argument in my head." This isn't a weakness;

it's a signal. Your nervous system is trying to protect you. Honor that, but don't obey it blindly.

Step 2: Interrupt the Pattern

Once you notice the loop, do something different, anything that shifts the energy.

Take a walk.

Call a friend.

Write down what you're feeling.

Breathe deeply for 60 seconds.

Go to the gym; work out.

The goal isn't to fix the emotion; it's to break the automatic behavior that reinforces it.

Step 3: Rewire Through New Choices

Dr. Dispenza's research shows that new choices create new emotions. So, we practiced choosing differently:

Instead of checking social media, Shelly wrote a letter to herself about what she deserved.

Instead of driving by the house, she drove to a new place she'd never explored.

Instead of wearing the ring, she bought a new one that symbolized her healing.

Each new choice sent a message to her brain: We're safe. We're moving forward. We're creating something new.

Step 4: Anchor in the Present

Loops keep you bound to the past, to what has already happened. Healing lives in the present. To anchor in the present, you can practice grounding techniques, touching something textured, naming five things in the room, breathing into the belly, to bring yourself into the here and now. I once put a hair band around my wrist and would pop it each time I found myself thinking about the past or worrying about the future. Freedom isn't hiding in what was or what will be, it's right here, in the present moment.

Rebuilding the Self After Identity Loss

Shelly's story mirrored something I had experienced myself. There was a time when I didn't know who I was outside of the roles I played, mother, wife, caretaker, and peacekeeper. I had built my identity around what others needed from me, not who I truly was. So, when relationships shifted or roles dissolved, I felt like I was disappearing. I wasn't just grieving people; I was grieving the version of myself that had been tied to them. Healing required more than letting go of others. It required rediscovering me.

1. Name the Roles You've Outgrown

Start by identifying the roles you've been living in that no longer serve you.

"I was the fixer."

"I was the one who kept the peace."

"I was the one who always said yes."

Naming them helps you begin to release them.

2. Ask: Who Am I Without That Role?

This question can feel terrifying, but it's also liberating. Who are you when you're not performing, pleasing, or protecting? Who are you when you're not defined by someone else's story?

3. Reconnect with Forgotten Desires

What did you love before life got heavy?
What lit you up before you started dimming your light for

others?

Make a list. Paint. Dance. Write. Travel. Dream again.

4. Create New Anchors of Identity

Instead of defining yourself by who you were to others, begin anchoring your identity in values, passions, and purpose.

"I am someone who values truth."

"I am someone who creates beauty."

"I am someone who shows up with compassion."

These anchors are internal. They can't be taken away.

5. Practice Being You in Safe Spaces

Start showing up as the real you, unfiltered, unmasked, in places where it's safe to be seen. That might mean sitting across from a therapist, confiding in a trusted friend, or even speaking your truth aloud when you're alone. Authenticity isn't a trait you're born with; it's a muscle. And like any muscle, it grows stronger with practice. Every time you choose honesty over hiding, you're teaching your nervous system that it's safe to be you.

The Addiction to Familiar Pain

Shelly said it, the thing that had been eating her alive. "We tried counseling for three years. Three years is a long time. If I let go now, what was all that work for? What if he finally gets it next month and makes a change? What if I give up right before the breakthrough?

I felt the weight of every word. Shelly wasn't just grieving a relationship; she was grieving years of effort, energy, and hope she'd never get back. This is what psychologists call the sunk cost fallacy: the belief that because you've poured so much into something, walking away would mean all of it was wasted.

But here's what I helped her see: those three years weren't wasted. They were her graduate degree in boundaries, self-worth, and emotional clarity. She had earned wisdom she could carry into every future relationship. The heartbreak wasn't meaningless; it was her education in what she would never accept again.

Yet the most heartbreaking part? Shelly was still waiting for the conversation that would make it all make sense. The explanation that would justify the pain. The apology that would provide closure. "If I could just understand why he chose her over me," she said, "then maybe I could finally move on."

That's when I realized: Shelly wasn't trying to heal. She was addicted to searching for answers. She had mistaken analysis for progress, believing that if she could just figure it out, she'd be free. But instead of moving forward, she was stuck in the familiar pain of "what if", avoiding the unfamiliar freedom of "what's next."

Releasing the Need for Closure

Shelly's story reminded me of something I had to learn the hard way: closure isn't something someone else gives you. It's something you create for yourself. Waiting for the perfect explanation, the apology that never comes, or the moment that finally "makes it all make sense" is like standing at a train station for a train that was canceled years ago, believing that if you wait, it will magically appear. The peace you're searching for won't come from answers; it comes from surrendering to what is because answers don't heal; acceptance does.

Here's the framework I use to help clients (and myself) release the need for closure:

1. Name What You're Waiting For

Start by identifying the specific thing you're hoping will happen.

"I want them to admit they were wrong."

"I want to understand why they chose someone else."

"I want to know if they ever really loved me."
Naming it helps you see the emotional hook that's keeping you stuck.

2. Ask: What Would That Give Me?

Then ask yourself: If I got that answer, what would it give me emotionally?

Relief?

Validation?

Permission to move on?
This helps you realize that it's not the answer you need; it's the emotional resolution.

3. Create Your Own Closure Statement

Write a statement that gives you the emotional permission you've been waiting for.

"I may never know why they left, but I know I deserve love."

"I release the need for their apology. I choose peace."

"I don't need their validation to know my worth."
This is your power reclaiming moment.

4. Ritualize the Release

Sometimes closure needs a physical act.

Write a letter and burn it.

Take off the ring.

Visit a place and say goodbye.

Rituals help the body and brain register that something has ended, and something new is beginning.

Reflection Exercise: Your Closure Conversation

Take a moment to complete these prompts:

The answer I've been waiting for is…

If I got that answer, I would feel…

What I really need to feel closure is…

My closure statement is…

My ritual for release will be…

The Ritual That Set Her Free

"Write him a letter," I told Shelly. "Not to send, but to release. Say everything you've been holding in. The hurt. The hope. The disappointment. All of it. Then you are going to burn it." She looked at me like I'd lost my mind. "That's so dramatic," she said, half-laughing, half-guarded. I smiled gently. "Your nervous system doesn't process healing through logic; it craves what feels alive: fire, ceremony, and embodied action."

If you want your body to believe it's over, you must show it through ritual." The next week, Shelly showed up to our call transformed. Her face was lighter. Her voice was steadier, and her energy was different. "I wrote seventeen pages," she said. "I had no idea I was carrying that much frustration and pain. When I watched it burn in my fireplace, something inside me let go. It was like I'd been holding my breath for two years and finally exhaled." That's the power of rituals. It bypasses logic and speaks directly to the body. It tells your nervous system: It's safe to let go now. The story is complete.

Create Your Own Release Ritual: A Step-by-Step Guide to Letting Go

Letting go isn't just a decision; it's a process your body, mind, and soul need to experience together. This ritual is designed to help you release emotional baggage, reclaim your energy, and create space for the life you're ready to live.

Step 1: Write It All Down

Let your truth spill onto the page.
Write a letter to the person, situation, or version of yourself you're ready to release. Include:

What hurt you.

What did you hope for?

What you've learned?

What are you choosing to let go of?

Tip: Don't edit or censor. This is for you, not for them.

Step 2: Read It Out Loud

Speak your truth. Hearing your own voice speak the words out loud helps your brain process the emotions and gives your nervous system permission to release. You could also record yourself reading it and listen back.

Step 3: Choose Your Ritual

Pick a physical action that symbolizes release. Your body needs to see and feel the letting go.

Burning – transformation through fire.

Burying – returning to the earth.

Water Release – letting emotions flow away.

Shredding – breaking apart what no longer serves you.

Choose what feels most powerful and personal.

Step 4: Witness the Release

Don't rush this part. Stay present. Watch the letter burn, sink, dissolve, or disappear. Let your body register and feel the shift. Breathe deeply. Feel the exhale. You're not abandoning the past; you're honoring it by letting it go.

Step 5: Fill the Space

Letting go creates space. Now fill it with something that reflects who you're becoming.

Choose one or more:

Write a letter to your future self.

Create a vision board for your next chapter.

Take a photo in a power pose and make it your wallpaper.

Apply for the job or program you've been afraid to pursue.

Rearrange your space, add plants, and create a sacred corner.

Update your wardrobe to reflect your true self.

Ask yourself:
What would have felt impossible while carrying the old baggage? Now do that. That's your proof of transformation.

Reflection Prompt

After your ritual, take time to journal:

What did I feel during the release?

What am I no longer available for?

What am I now free to create, pursue, or become?

The 37-Year Run

The Freedom on the Other Side

Nine months later, Shelly was unrecognizable, not just happier but profoundly transformed. She had reclaimed her life in ways she never thought possible. She started rock climbing. She joined a book club, traveled to Italy alone, and began dating someone who saw her worth from the very beginning.

During our final session, she shared a moment that marked her full-circle healing.

"I ran into David last week at the grocery store," she said. "And for the first time in three years, I looked at him and felt nothing. Not love. Not hate. Not hope. Just nothing." I asked gently, "How did that feel?" She paused, tears welling in her eyes. "Freeing," she whispered. "But here's the thing, I realized I wasn't grieving him anymore. I was celebrating who I'd become without him."

A year later, Shelly sent me a photo from her wedding, not to David, but to a man who had loved her fully from their very first date. A man who never asked her to prove her worth or earn his commitment. A man who met her where she was and honored who she had become.

Why Letting Go Feels Like Death

Letting go feels terrifying for a reason, because on a neurological level, it is a kind of death. It's the death of who you used to be. The death of dreams that will never come to pass. The death of the version of your story you thought you were living.

Watching Shelly and so many others move through this process taught me something profound: death and rebirth are the natural cycles of growth and renewal. You cannot become who you're meant to be while clinging to the old version of yourself.

Research shows that trying to bypass the natural stages of grief doesn't speed up healing; it prolongs suffering. The original five stages of grief still apply, even when what you're grieving isn't a person, but a version of yourself or a life you thought you'd have:

Denial: "This isn't really over."

Anger: "How could they do this to me?"

Bargaining: "What if I try harder?"

Depression: "I'll never love again."

Acceptance: "I'm ready for what's next.

When You Clear the Space, Everything Shifts

The beautiful irony is that when you truly let go, when you stop clinging, stop bargaining, stop waiting, you create space for either a genuine second chance or something infinitely better.

Shelly spent three years begging David to come to counseling, to stop drinking, to choose their marriage over his addiction. She twisted herself into knots trying to love him back to health, while he repeatedly chose the bottle over their future. The moment she stopped fighting for a man who wouldn't fight for himself, everything shifted. Six months after their divorce was final, Shelly met Michael at a coffee shop. She was reading alone for the first time in years, something David had always mocked as "antisocial." Michael noticed her book, asked about it, and listened to her answer like her voice mattered.

Her marriage to Michael works not because she got a second chance with the wrong person, but because she finally made space for the right one. It's built on mutual respect and authentic love, not desperate hope and one-sided effort. The universe had been waiting for her to clear out the chaos David had been occupying. And once she did, everything changed.

The 37-Year Run

The Runway Is Cleared for Takeoff

The second chance was never about them. It was always about you, getting a second chance at life, at love, at dreams, at becoming who you were always meant to be. The moment you stop settling for less than you desire, everything begins to shift.

Here's what the research doesn't often tell you about letting go: your nervous system will fight you every step of the way. It will interpret release as abandonment, change as danger, and growth as threat. Your brain was designed to keep you alive, not to keep you thriving. It would rather you stay miserable and safe than happy and uncertain. But your soul knows better.

Your soul knows this: every release is a rebirth. Every letting go is a doorway to something new. Every death of the old self cracks open the possibility of life again. Your nervous system doesn't heal through logic; it responds to what feels alive. Letting go will feel like dying. It will burn. It will ache. But the real question is this: will you walk through the fire that leads to resurrection, or stay in the ashes of what's already gone?

As we close this chapter, pause and listen: is something in your life whispering to be released? A relationship that's run its course. A dream that's become a cage. A version of yourself you've outgrown. You can feel it, the ache of holding on when your soul longs to open. The life you desire isn't waiting for perfection; it's waiting for courage. Courage to loosen your grip. Courage to trust the unknown.

Your second chance begins the moment you choose yourself. Let go. The holding pattern is over. It's time to rise into light, into freedom, into the life that's been calling your name all along.

CHAPTER TEN

Serial Quitter to Dream Finisher

Why Momentum Beats Motivation Every Single Time

I was forty-six years old, standing nearly naked on a stage in front of hundreds of strangers, when I realized I was about to do what I'd done my entire adult life: run away the moment courage was required. My body trembled so intensely that I could barely hold my poses. Under the heat of the lights, the spray tan clung to my skin like armor, and the metallic taste of fear coated my tongue, a familiar signal that I was stepping into something far beyond my comfort zone.

The crowd had gone quiet. Not the kind of quiet that means you've captivated them, but the kind that means you're failing publicly. Every muscle in my body screamed the same old chorus: "Leave. Just walk off the stage. Pretend you're sick. Make up an excuse. Do what you always do when things get hard." And then, in the middle of that moment, I had the most important conversation of my life, with myself. "Don't quit on yourself again, Valerie. You've spent your entire adult life abandoning your dreams the moment they required real courage. Not this time."

That word, run, hit me like a punch to the gut. Because this wasn't the first time I'd stood on the edge of something meaningful and chosen to walk away. It was just the latest in a decades-long pattern of self-abandonment that had cost me everything I claimed to want. I had lived as a serial quitter. And this moment, this stage, this spotlight, was my last stand.

The 37-Year Run

What I hadn't told anyone, and could barely admit to myself, was how deeply I'd come to resent the woman I'd become. Not the survivor of trauma, not the woman who escaped an abusive marriage with her soul intact. No, it was the version of me who couldn't trust herself to finish what she started. By forty-six, I was carrying the silent weight of a thousand abandoned dreams. Each unfinished project, each half-hearted goal, every moment I'd chosen comfort over courage had etched a cruel belief into my bones: I was unreliable, even to myself. The shame didn't just live in my mind; it settled into my body like a second skin. When people asked about my education, my chest would tighten. When conversations drifted toward long-term plans, I'd skillfully steer them elsewhere. Compliments about my potential felt like daggers wrapped in silk. I'd laugh them off, knowing deep down that potential was all I'd ever offer. I had become an expert at starting something and a master of quitting just before the breakthrough. And that truth haunted me more than any past I'd survived.

Dream #1: Physical Therapy Career

After my second child, I enrolled in a physical therapy program with genuine excitement and undeniable aptitude. When I was accepted into the clinical phase, an hour-and-a-half drive to Galveston, I felt something I hadn't felt since becoming a mother: myself. Capable, intelligent, and purposeful.

Then came his verdict: "No. I won't allow it." It wasn't about money or logistics. It was control dressed as concern. "I won't allow you to drive to another city for school," he said. But what he meant was, "I need you small and dependent."

I quit without protest, without negotiation. What I didn't understand then was that I wasn't just surrendering to his control. I was abandoning myself before anyone else could. His refusal to support my dreams became the blueprint for how I'd treat myself for years.

I told myself I was being a good wife, a devoted mother. But what I was really doing was training my nervous system to believe my dreams were dangerous, my desires selfish, that wanting more than what I was given made me ungrateful. I wasn't just giving up a career; I was giving up the right to want, the right to grow into who I was created to become.

Dream #2: Business Degree

Fine, I thought. I'll choose something less threatening. I pivoted to a business degree, practical, respectable, and, most importantly, less likely to provoke his jealousy. I worked hard, made progress, and was halfway through the program when he delivered another blow: "You can't work anywhere that employs men. I won't have my wife around other men all day."

The nausea that rose in my stomach wasn't just disappointing; it was recognition. I was married to someone who would dismantle every path to my fulfillment. And I had learned to let him. So, I quit. I told myself it was for the good of our marriage. But once again, I trained my brain to prioritize his control over my growth, and his comfort over my autonomy. Each time I walked away from a dream, I wasn't just losing a future; I was reinforcing a belief that my freedom was negotiable.

Dream #3: Teaching Career

Eventually, he offered a compromise. "You can become a schoolteacher," he said, as if granting permission for dreams he deemed appropriately feminine. "That's acceptable." I agreed, but my heart wasn't in it. It felt like settling, not choosing. It felt like surviving, not living. And I was tired, tired of fighting for scraps of my own life. So, I quit that too. By then, the pattern was so deeply ingrained that I didn't need his voice to silence me. I had internalized it so completely that I could abandon myself without his help. Each time I gave up, I carved a deeper groove into the story I believed about myself: that I wasn't someone who could finish, that I wasn't built for persistence, that I was only good at beginnings. And the shame of that belief became heavier than any failure.

Undoing the Damage

What I didn't know then was that I was living inside a psychological phenomenon known as learned helplessness, a condition where repeated exposure to uncontrollable circumstances teaches the brain to stop trying, even when escape or change becomes possible. Dr. Martin Seligman's research revealed that when efforts consistently fail to produce results, the brain rewires itself to expect defeat. The neural pathways responsible for persistence and problem-solving begin to atrophy, while those linked to avoidance and resignation grow stronger. But here's the deeper truth that took me decades to uncover: living with someone who systematically undermines your goals isn't just emotionally corrosive, it's neurologically damaging. My brain had been trained to interpret my own desires as threats. Every time I quit to avoid his anger, I was teaching my nervous system that ambition was dangerous. Every time I settled for peace instead of pursuing purpose, I reinforced the lie that conflict would destroy me, and disappointment was more than I could handle. By the time I left my marriage, I wasn't just rebuilding a life; I was retraining a brain that had learned to flinch at the very thought of persistence.

A Journey Through Change

I didn't rewrite my story in one sweeping act. There was no lightning bolt of clarity, no cinematic breakthrough. It began quietly in whispers, in microscopic acts of defiance against the version of me that had learned to disappear.

I didn't wake up one morning, brimming with confidence. I woke up tired, aching, and unsure of myself, but still willing to put in the work. And that willingness was everything in my self-help journey.

The first step wasn't glamorous. It was learning to sit with discomfort instead of sprinting away from it. To allow myself to feel the things that I had spent years outrunning and to allow the heartache to speak.

I started small. When a task felt impossible, when a conversation felt too vulnerable, when a dream felt too big, I paused. I breathed. I stayed. That pause became my rebellion. It was the neurological equivalent of planting a flag in new territory.

Then came the science. I discovered neuroplasticity, the brain's ability to rewire itself, and for the first time, hope wasn't just a feeling. It was a function. I told myself if my brain had learned helplessness, it could learn resilience.

I began small and started practicing courage in small doses: speaking up, making the phone call I'd been avoiding, setting a boundary without apologizing. Each act, no matter how small, was a vote for the person I was becoming. Slowly, the wiring shifted. The voice that once echoed with doubt grew quieter. In its place, a new voice emerged. A voice that said, "You can do hard things, you can finish, and you are not broken; you are rebuilding."

The Three Rounds That Rebuilt My Soul

What happened on that stage wasn't just a competition. This was my first bikini bodybuilding show. I signed up for three categories that would perform back-to-back, and I was terrified.

The 37-Year Run

Stepping out there became more than a moment; it became the blueprint for every challenge I would face, from that day forward.

Round One: In heels that felt like stilts, my legs shook so violently I nearly fell before reaching center stage. The lights hit me like an interrogation, exposing every fear, every doubt, every voice that said I didn't belong here. I turned in the wrong direction and missed my first pose completely. Barely hit the back pose. I could hear the confusion rippling through the audience, not cruel whispers, just puzzled ones, wondering what this forty-six-year-old woman was doing on stage, so clearly unprepared for this moment.

My body betrayed me in every possible way. Muscles I'd trained for months refused to cooperate. My mind went blank. The routine I'd practiced a couple of hundred times evaporated. Every survival instinct I'd developed over the years screamed the same command: Run! However, my feet didn't listen as they stayed planted. I fumbled through the rest of the routine; graceless, disoriented, probably the worst performance those judges had ever seen. When I finally walked off that stage, something inside me had shifted. For the first time in my life, I didn't abandon myself when things got messy. I stayed. And staying changed everything.

Round Two: Back on stage. Still trembling, but now it was manageable, like aftershocks instead of the earthquake. This time, when the lights hit bright, I didn't flinch. I managed something that might have been a smile. The routine came back to me in pieces, not perfect, but I felt my body was present. I hit my poses with actual intention instead of blind panic. Somewhere between the first turn and the last, I realized I wasn't just surviving anymore. I was participating. I was fully there, letting strangers see me struggle and improving in that moment. The voice screaming "run" softened to a whisper.

Valerie Maksym

Round Three:

No shaking as I walked to center stage; I felt like I belonged there. When I looked up at the judges, I didn't see executioners; I saw witnesses. Witnesses to what happens when a forty-six-year-old woman decides to stop hiding. My smile was genuine this time, not for them, but for me. Every pose, every turn, every movement came from a place I did not know existed; a place where you are your true self in front of others, unedited and unafraid. The end results stunned everyone, especially me: I received last place in round one. Middle to the end of the pack in round two. Then, in round three, I placed first.

However, those numbers didn't show the entire story. Backstage between each round, when I could have walked away, and I wanted to; I was having the most important conversation of my life with myself. I told myself, "This is what it feels like to stay and not quit when things get hard. This is what happens when you stop running. This is who you are when you stop performing and start living." The trophy was terrific, but the transformation was everything.

The M.O.M.E.N.T.U.M. Method: Breaking the Quit Cycle

Standing on that stage, terrified but refusing to run, I discovered something that would save my life over and over again: the exact moment when quitting becomes a choice, not a reflex.

In those three rounds, from paralyzed to present to powerful, my body taught me what my mind had been too afraid to learn. Every time I wanted to run but stayed, every time my legs shook but kept standing, every time shame screamed but I smiled anyway, I was building something I'd never had before: evidence that I could trust myself.

That night birthed the M.O.M.E.N.T.U.M. Method, an eight-step roadmap for breaking through when every cell in your body is begging you to give up. This isn't just another framework. This is the blueprint that taught a woman who ran for years how to stand tall and fight for herself.

These eight steps are what stand between the person you are when you want to quit and the person you become when you don't.

M – Make the Decision to Stay

This is the moment everything changes. Not a wish, not hope; a declaration. Say it out loud, even if your voice shakes: "I'm not running this time." Feel how those words change your body. Your spine straightens. Your feet root. You just drew a line in the sand between who you were and who you're becoming.

O – Observe the Urge to Quit

Your body will revolt. Mine did; my chest tightening like a fist, hands and legs trembling, that familiar voice hissing: "Everyone can see you're failing." Don't fight these sensations. Study them like a scientist. Where does the urge to run live in your body? What lie does it whisper? Name it, because unnamed fears own you.

M – Minimize the Next Step

Forget the finish line; it's too far away to help you now. Shrink your world to the next ten seconds. Not "finish this competition," but "lift your right arm." Not "save your marriage," but "have one honest conversation." Make it so small that even your fear can't argue with it.

E – Embrace the Discomfort

Here's the truth that changed everything: discomfort isn't your enemy, it's your teacher. That burning in your chest? That's expansion. That shaking? That's old patterns dying. Stop treating growth like an emergency. The discomfort is proof you're alive, not evidence you're failing.

N – Name Your Why

When everything screams quit, you need an anchor deeper than fear. Not "I want to win," but "I refuse to abandon myself again." Not "I need to succeed," but "My children are watching me choose." Find the why that makes you willing to burn for it.

T – Take One More Action

Perfection is not required. Courage is. Even if you're crying, even if you're the worst one there, do the next thing. Move your body. Speak the truth. Stay in the room. Action is the antidote to fear, and momentum is born from the smallest movement forward.

U – Use Each Success to Build

You're not just completing tasks; you're collecting evidence of who you really are. Every time you stay, you're rewriting your identity: I am someone who doesn't quit. Stack these moments like bricks. You're building a foundation that fear can't shake.

M – Multiply the Pattern

This isn't a one-time rescue. It's a practice that becomes a way of life. The stage becomes the boardroom becomes the difficult conversation becomes the dream you've been afraid to chase. Each time you use this method, you're strengthening the muscle that keeps you standing when everything inside you wants to give up and quit.

This method saved me on that bodybuilding stage. Then it saved me in my relationships, my mindset, in my business, and in my love life. Now it's yours to put into practice as well.

The 37-Year Run

The Trophy That Broke Me Open

That night, I sat alone in my car holding a first-place trophy I never expected to win and did something I hadn't done in years: I counted the cost. Not in dollars or opportunities; those losses were easy to calculate. I counted in abandoned dreams, in half-finished journals, in business cards for careers that ended before they had a chance to get fully launched. I counted the times I'd introduced myself as "trying to be" instead of "I am." Every quit had left a scar, and sitting there in the parking lot, I finally let myself feel them all.

When was the last time you sat with your own quitting? Really sat with it? The grief hit first, for the woman who spent years believing she was fundamentally broken, incapable of finishing anything that mattered. Then came the rage, raw and overdue, at everyone who had taught me that my dreams came with asterisks, that wanting more was selfish, that staying small was safer.

But then something shifted. In that dark car, the trophy in my lap, I felt something I'd never allowed myself before: compassion for the quitter. She hadn't been weak; she'd been terrified. Every time she ran, she was protecting herself from the humiliation of being seen trying and failing. Every quit was a preemptive strike against disappointment. She wasn't lazy. She was traumatized. And trauma teaches you that the safest thing to do when things get hard is to disappear.

The woman who quit a thousand times didn't need my contempt. She needed my understanding. The threats that made her run; the criticism, the judgment, the fear of not being enough; they were all ghosts now. And in their absence, one truth emerged with devastating clarity: I was the only one left who could abandon her. After all these years, I had become my own worst threat. That night, I made a vow that changed everything: I would never be her enemy again.

Why Motivation Is a Liar and Momentum Is Truth

A few years after my first competition, I discovered research that explained what had happened to me on that stage. Dr. BJ Fogg at Stanford had mapped out something that made my transformation make sense: the profound difference between motivation and momentum.

Here's what nobody tells you about motivation: it's a liar. Motivation whispers sweet promises when you're comfortable, then vanishes the moment things get hard. It's loudest when you're planning and silent when you're struggling. It depends entirely on how you feel, and feelings, as any survivor knows, are unreliable narrators. Think about it: How many times have you waited to "feel ready" before starting something that mattered?

Momentum is different. Momentum doesn't care how you feel. While motivation is emotional and fleeting, momentum is mechanical and unstoppable. It's not built on inspiration; it's built on action. One foot in front of the other. One more rep when your body says stop, and one more sentence when the page stays blank. Momentum grows stronger under pressure while motivation crumbles. It feeds on resistance while motivation flees from it.

Here's what blew my mind: studies reveal brain scans showing this happening. Every time you push through the urge to quit, you're literally rewiring your anterior cingulate cortex, the part of your brain that governs persistence and resilience. You're not just making a choice; you're becoming a different person at the cellular level. Someone who stays. Someone who finishes. Someone who can trust themselves. For forty-six years, I waited to feel motivated before taking action. I had it completely

The 37-Year Run

backward. You don't get motivated and then take action. You take action; messy, imperfect, terrified action, and watch as the momentum builds. Motivation eventually shows up, late and taking credit, like it was there all along.

What would change in your life if you stopped waiting to feel ready? The woman who walked onto that stage wasn't motivated. She was terrified. But she took one step, then another, and momentum caught her. Three rounds later, she was holding proof that everything she believed about herself was wrong. That's not motivation. That's momentum.

The Ripple Effect of Keeping Promises

Every time I finished something, anything, I wasn't just checking a box. I was becoming living proof that I could trust myself. For the first time in my life, I became someone who kept her word, starting with the promises I made to myself. That transformation didn't stay contained. It spread like light. My children watched as I transformed before their eyes, not in some dramatic overnight miracle, but in the daily evidence of follow-through. They watched me write my first book. They watched me build a business from idea to income. They watched me step on stage for eight consecutive years, each time a little stronger, a little less afraid. But here's what really changed: they stopped seeing a mother who was always "about to" or "trying to." They started seeing a woman who finishes what she starts. And that permission to complete, to commit, to trust yourself became their inheritance.

My marriage transformed, too. John had fallen in love with a woman who was always starting over; new diets, new projects, new versions of herself that never lasted long. Now he was married to someone who followed through. The frantic energy of perpetual beginnings gave way to something more profound: the quiet confidence of a woman who knows she'll show up tomorrow for what she started today. Anxiety left our home. Stability moved in.

Here's what nobody tells you: when you stop abandoning yourself, everyone around you feels safer. Your completion creates permission for others to complete. Your commitment teaches others that they can commit. Your transformation doesn't just change you; it changes everyone who's watching, everyone who's counting on you, everyone who's been waiting for proof that change is possible.

The woman who stays creates a different world than the woman who runs. Even my inner dialogue changed. The voice that once whispered, "You give up when things get hard," was replaced with a new truth: "You finish what matters." That identity shift didn't just change my behavior; it changed my belief system. And from that belief, everything else began to bloom.

Your Last Stand Moment

Right now, you might be standing on your own stage, a struggling business, a relationship that requires work, a dream demanding more of you than you thought you had to give. You have the same choice I had in that moment of fear: to run or to stay. To quit or to finish. And the truth is, the urge to quit is the strongest right before the breakthrough. Your brain will whisper that discomfort is dangerous, and that difficulty means you're failing. But it doesn't. It means you're growing.

Ask yourself: Am I quitting because it's impossible or because it's uncomfortable? What would the person I desire to become do in this moment? This is your last stand-off moment. The one where you decide whether you live a life of almost and what-ifs or a life of completed goals and unshakable self-respect. Stop chasing motivation; it will abandon you when you need it most.

The 37-Year Run

Start building momentum; it will carry you when motivation fails.

Don't walk away from yourself, not this time. You've done that enough for one lifetime. Your dreams are waiting just beyond the struggle you've been avoiding. All you have to do is stay. Stay when it hurts. Stay when it feels impossible. Stay when every fiber of you wants to run. The crowd is watching. The judges are ready. This is your moment. Stay in it. Fight for it. Finish what you started. Your future self is counting on you.

CHAPTER ELEVEN

From "All Men Cheat" to "Faithful Love Exists"

From Speaking Limitations to Creating Possibilities

I was sitting in my car, mascara streaking down my cheeks, stunned from a phone call that shattered my world. My boyfriend of two years had just confessed to cheating. Looking back, the signs were all there: flirty messages with other women, secret plans made behind my back, and all the lies I was too trusting to question. But it wasn't the betrayal that haunted me for the next three years. It was what I said next. "All men cheat." I didn't whisper it. I yelled it out loud, raw, broken, and furious. My voice cracked under the weight of every disappointment, every broken promise, and every time I had chosen to trust and been punished for it. In that moment of devastation, I unknowingly planted a belief that would shape my reality. I had activated what psychologists call confirmation bias, the tendency to seek out and interpret evidence that supports your existing beliefs. However, I wasn't just confirming my beliefs; I was building a mental prison, and I was locking myself inside.

The Weight of Words I Couldn't Take Back

That moment in the car didn't end when the tears dried; it echoed far beyond that day. The words I yelled out didn't just fill the air; they dropped anchor in my chest, heavy and immovable. "All men cheat." It became more than a reaction; it became a belief. And beliefs, especially those born of pain, have a way of shaping everything that follows.

The 37-Year Run

Every time I considered dating again, those three words resurfaced like a warning. I didn't realize it then, but they were quietly rewriting my approach to love. Within weeks, I found myself scanning every man's behavior for signs of betrayal. A delayed text became evidence. Working late was a cover story. A casual chat with a waitress turned into a threat I needed to monitor. I had become a detective in my own love life, and the verdict was always the same: guilty. But here's what I couldn't see at the time. I wasn't just protecting myself from heartbreak. I was building walls so high that even the faithful couldn't climb them.

The Neuroscience of Self-Fulfilling Prophecies

What happened in my brain the moment I made that declaration was both fascinating and devastating. Dr. Joe Dispenza explains that when we repeatedly cycle through the same thoughts and emotions, we train our neural pathways to anticipate the same outcomes. In other words, I wasn't just reacting to heartbreak; I was programming my brain to relive every abandonment I'd ever survived.

I had unknowingly trapped myself in what researchers call a cognitive-emotional loop:

Declaration: All men cheat.

Expectation: I anticipate betrayal from every man I meet.

Emotion: I feel guarded, suspicious, and hypervigilant.

Behavior: I attract emotionally unavailable men or sabotage relationships with available ones.

Experience: Men behave badly or leave, confirming my belief.

Reinforcement: See? I was right. All men cheat.

The loop was complete. Sadly, I was locked inside it, using my own dating disasters as proof that my toxic belief was truth, rather than a self-imposed limitation.

When Life Became My Evidence Collection Agency

After I made that declaration, something strange began to happen. It felt like the universe had hired a team of investigators to prove me right. Evidence of betrayal began to appear everywhere. My streaming recommendations turned into Betrayal University, offering shows and movies centered around infidelity and broken trust. Love stories lost their innocence. I zeroed in on the one moment of temptation, the single glance, the lingering pause. That was all it took to confirm my belief that betrayal was everywhere.

Conversations with friends became confirmation sessions. Every story of suspicion, heartbreak, or betrayal added another layer to my belief. When someone shared a joyful moment in their relationship, I'd quietly dismiss it with thoughts like, "Just wait and see," or "She doesn't know what he's really like." Dating felt more like a crime scene investigation than a connection. I developed a signature approach to first dates: less conversation, more interrogation.

Asking questions like:

"What ended your last serious relationship?"

"Have you ever been unfaithful?"

"How do I know you're not like every other unfaithful guy?"

When someone shared their own story of betrayal, it didn't soothe me; it sealed my belief. See? I was right. Everyone cheats.

The 37-Year Run

The Power of a Pattern Interrupted

Three years into my "all men cheat" era, I was venting after yet another disappointing date when a friend said something that stopped me mid-sentence. "You need to stop saying that." I blinked, thrown off. "Wait, saying what?" "That all men cheat. You've been declaring that for years and look where it's gotten you. You're not only describing your present reality, you're also creating it." I braced to argue for my 'realistic' view, but her voice pressed forward, calm, firm, and impossible to ignore.

"Think about it. You've pushed away genuinely good men because you couldn't see their faithfulness through the lens of your fear. And you keep attracting the ones who confirm your belief. Your words aren't just reflections, they're instructions." Her words hit me like a splash of cold water on my face, shocking and impossible to ignore. For the first time in three years, I paused. Not to defend. Not to justify. But to consider the possibility that maybe, just maybe, the problem wasn't men. Perhaps it was the belief I'd been feeding myself. Maybe it was me.

The Science Behind Words That Wound

While some claims about the power of words have been exaggerated or misunderstood, solid research confirms that our internal narratives shape our experiences in measurable ways. Studies on cognitive bias reveal that when we hold strong negative beliefs about people, outcomes, or ourselves, we're more likely to:

Notice information that confirms those beliefs, while ignoring anything that contradicts them.

Interpret ambiguous situations in ways that support our assumptions.

Make choices that unconsciously create the very outcomes we expect.

In other words, our beliefs act as filters, shaping our reality. Harvard psychologist Dr. Ellen Langer has shown that individuals who use empowering language and hold positive expectations experience measurable improvements in performance, relationships, and overall well-being. (Langer & Ellen, 2009) Our words aren't magic spells, but they are powerful instructions to the brain, telling it what to look for, what to expect, and how to interpret the world around us.

There's a verse in the Bible that says, "The tongue has the power of life and death, and those who love it will eat its fruit." (Proverbs 18:21, NIV) It's a timeless reminder: what we speak can either build or break, heal or harm. Eventually, the world around us becomes the echo of our own words.

When New Words Create New Possibilities

The change in my belief that all men cheat wasn't immediate or magical, but it was undeniable. My media diet changed naturally. Instead of binging shows about affairs and betrayal, I found myself drawn to stories about enduring love. My algorithms started suggesting films that celebrated commitment rather than documenting its destruction. Conversations took on new flavors. The same friends who'd once shared relationship horror stories were now pointing out their partners' thoughtful gestures. Maybe they'd always said those things, but for the first time, I was able to hear them, choosing to notice the good instead of zeroing in on the bad. Sarah mentioned how Mark brought her coffee every morning. Jessica talked about Tom's love notes he put in her lunch. Lisa shared that her husband still opens doors for her after fifteen years of being together. Had their relationships suddenly improved? No. I'd started listening to and interpreting what they would say differently. Dating

The 37-Year Run

became a discovery, not an investigation. Instead of interrogating men about betrayals, I started asking: "What does commitment mean to you?" "How do you show someone you care?" "What excites you about building a life with someone?" By doing this, the quality of conversations and men had completely transformed.

The Man My New Words Made Room For

Six months after changing my declaration, I met someone new. Our first date was at a cozy restaurant near my apartment, nothing extravagant, but something felt different. When the conversation turned to past relationships, I asked a question I'd never asked before: *"What was the best part of your previous relationships?"* His answer shifted something in me. He spoke with genuine kindness and respect, acknowledging that relationships can end without blame or betrayal. *"Sometimes people just grow in different directions,"* he said thoughtfully. *"That doesn't make either person bad."* No cheating. No drama. Just a man who understood that endings don't always require destruction, sometimes they simply require honesty. *"That's refreshing,"* I said, realizing I'd never heard someone speak about relationship endings with such grace. And for the first time in years, when he asked what I wanted in a relationship, I didn't mention anything about betrayal or heartbreak. I said, "The freedom to be the best version of myself, not to be reshaped into something I'm not. I'm looking for someone who complements me, not completes. Because I believe when two whole people come together, that's not just a formula for love, that's the recipe for a power couple." His eyes lit up. *"That's exactly what I believe, as well."*

The Work Beyond Words

Changing the words I spoke was only the beginning. I had to retrain my eyes to see the green flags I'd been conditioned to ignore, the quiet signs of respect and reliability. The small things, like calling when he said he would. Inviting me into his world instead of leaving me on the sidelines and following through on promises while showing up emotionally, without hiding behind mystery.

As the relationship progressed, I had to practice believing his faithfulness was absolute, not an act. I had to learn how to sit with trust instead of defaulting to suspicion. Rewiring years of hypervigilance into healthy awareness wasn't easy. It wasn't just about positive thinking; it was about healing the parts of me that braced for abandonment. It meant facing the trauma that made betrayal feel inevitable. And it meant becoming someone who could not only recognize healthy love but also sustain it.

Your Declaration Audit

Words carry weight. They don't just reflect what we think; they shape what we believe, often rooted in unhealed wounds and inherited narratives, quietly influencing the choices we make and the stories we tell ourselves. Take a moment to complete these sentences with whatever comes to mind first:

All men _____.

All women _____.

I always _____.

I never _____.

Love is _____.

I'm not the type of person who _____.

Now, pause and ask yourself:

Where did these declarations come from?

What evidence have I been collecting to support them?

The 37-Year Run

How might these words limit my possibilities?

What would I prefer to experience instead?

The beliefs that feel most "true" are often the ones quietly holding you back. This isn't about judgment; it's about awareness, because once you see the script, you can start rewriting it and create a life that reflects your deepest values, not your old limitations.

The Love My New Words Made Possible

Today, I'm married to a man who has never once given me a reason to question his faithfulness. He includes me in every part of his life and speaks about our future with the quiet certainty of someone who means what he says. Sometimes I catch myself marveling at his consistency, not because it's extraordinary, but because I spent so many years believing it was impossible.

The woman who once screamed "all men cheat" in her car wouldn't have recognized this kind of love, let alone received it. She was too busy building walls to notice someone trying to build a bridge. But the woman who chose to declare "faithful men exist" created space for a love she'd never known before.

I didn't just change my words; I changed my capacity to recognize love. To attract it. To sustain it. The relationship I once sabotaged with fear is now the one I nurture with trust. And it all began with a new declaration.

The Power You've Always Had

Your words aren't magic; they are powerful instructions to your unconscious mind. They shape what you seek, what you expect, and what you allow into your life. Every declaration is a seed planted in the soil of your future experiences. "I always fail" grows into a garden of abandoned dreams. "Love never lasts" cultivates relationships with expiration dates. "I'm not good enough" attracts people who treat you as if you aren't.

But here's the truth:

The same power that creates limitations can create breakthroughs.

The same voice that speaks defeat can speak victory. The same mind that expects betrayal can learn to expect faithfulness. You've always had the power. Now you finally know how to use it.

The Question That Changes Everything

Right now, in this moment, ask yourself: What reality have my words been creating? And what reality do I want them to create instead? The man I might have loved never stood a chance, not while I clung to the belief that "all men cheat." My cynicism was a bouncer at the door of my heart, turning away anyone who dared to prove me wrong. The love I know today exists because I fired that bouncer. I rewrote the script. I shifted my expectations. And in doing so, I changed my life.

Your declarations haven't just described your world; they've been designing it. Every time you've said, "I can't," "I'm not," or "They always," you've sent instructions to your brain about what reality to build. But here's the truth that changes everything: If your words have created your current reality, they can also create a different one.

Your Next Declaration

You have a choice. You can keep repeating the words that have kept you small, safe, and separate from the life you truly desire. Or you can begin speaking about the reality you're ready to live in. Not because words are magic, but because they are the blueprint for transformation. They shape what you notice. They shift what you expect. They influence who you become. Your next declaration is waiting. Your new reality is listening. What will you choose to speak into existence?

The 37-Year Run

The love, the joy, the success, the healing, they're all waiting on the other side of the words you've been afraid to speak. Stop declaring your limitations. Start declaring your possibilities. Your life is listening to you. And it's ready to rise to everything you're bold enough to believe.

CHAPTER TWELVE

Stop Asking Why, Start Protecting Who

The Painting That Changed Everything

I was wandering through a small art gallery, when a massive painting stopped me mid-step. The 3D painting looked so realistic. It had five climbers ascending Mt. Everest; their bodies bent at impossible angles against winds that seemed to scream off the canvas. The artist had captured something visceral, ice crystals whipping horizontally across their faces; visibility reduced to mere feet, and every foothold looked like a gamble between progress and disaster. The summit was invisible, swallowed by clouds that looked like they could devour a person whole.

The woman beside me spoke of the painting as reality as she gasped. "Oh my, how horrible," she whispered to her husband, clutching his arm. "They look like they are immensely suffering. I'd turn around immediately; no summit is worth that misery." She shuddered. "What a horrifying way to die." Her husband nodded. "It's a foolish risk in my opinion. They should turn around."

I stood there, staring at the same canvas, seeing something completely different. Where she saw suffering, I saw strength. Look at their posture, not the hunched collapse of defeat, but the deliberate lean of climbers who knew how to work with the mountain, not against it. Everything about their equipment exuded preparation, not panic; each piece positioned exactly where it needed to be for survival. Ice axes planted with precision. Ropes taut with purpose. These weren't amateur thrill-seekers caught in a death trap. These were seasoned climbers who'd probably summited a dozen peaks before attempting the ultimate one.

The woman kept talking, her voice rising with each observation. "They must be terrified. Look how small they are against that storm. They're probably lost. They're going to freeze to death up there." She turned to another gallery visitor. "Can you imagine? I'd be crying, begging to go down. No view is worth dying for." As she was speaking, I couldn't stop studying their body language. There was no panic in their movements. No hesitation in their formation. They were lined up in perfect formation; each climber maintaining perfect spacing; close enough to help, far enough to avoid creating danger for each other. The lead climber's stance radiated confidence, even through the blizzard. This wasn't their first storm. Maybe not even their worst one. "It's like watching a suicide," the woman continued, now addressing anyone who would listen. "Why would anyone choose this torture?"

That's when it hit me, we were looking at the exact same painting but living in completely different worlds. She saw victims of circumstance, people who'd made a terrible mistake and were paying for it. I saw warriors who'd trained for this moment, who understood that the storm wasn't their enemy; it was their teacher. Every brutal gust of wind was making them stronger, more capable, more alive than those of us standing comfortably in climate-controlled galleries could ever be. The storm wasn't something happening to them. They had prepared for it, possibly even welcomed it. Because they knew something that woman didn't: The mountain doesn't care about your fear. It only reveals who you really are.

I thought about all the storms in my own life. The ones I'd run from, the ones that had flattened me, the ones I'd barely survived. What if I'd been looking at them wrong this entire time? What if the storm wasn't the problem?

The woman and her husband moved on, muttering about "death wish" and "insanity." I stayed, captivated by the beautiful painting. We were looking at the same painting, the same storm, and the same climbers fighting through impossible conditions. And we told ourselves two completely different stories. In her story, they were casualties waiting to happen. In mine, they were exactly where they'd trained to be, doing exactly what they'd prepared to do, becoming exactly who they were meant to become.

In that moment of reflection, my takeaway was that it's not only what happens to you in life that determines your outcome. It's the meaning you assign to what happens in life. Just like in the painting, the storm is the same. But whether it defeats you or defines you? That's entirely up to you.

The Meaning That Nearly Destroyed Me

I stood in that gallery for another twenty minutes after the woman left, unable to move, because I'd just seen my own story in those climbers, except I'd been reading it all wrong.

Three years earlier, I'd discovered the man I'd spent two years planning a future with had been cheating the entire time. The betrayal cut so deep I couldn't breathe, couldn't function, couldn't imagine trusting again. The evidence had unraveled fast. The "work trips." The phone tilted away. The answer that gutted me: all of it had been a lie. Every moment. The entire relationship had been fiction.

For three years, I didn't just avoid dating, I hid from it. Love felt like standing at the base of Mt. Everest in shorts and sandals. Impossible. Deadly. Ridiculous to even consider. But standing in that gallery, I finally saw the truth: It wasn't his betrayal that had trapped me. It was the story I'd written about it. Like that woman seeing only death in the climbers, I'd looked at his cheating and saw only one meaning: I wasn't enough.

If only I'd been prettier, more outgoing, more successful then maybe then he wouldn't have strayed. I became a detective investigating my own inadequacy, examining every memory for evidence of my failure. That time I was too busy to show up for him, was that when he decided I wasn't worth faithful love? The argument about not being allowed to see his phone, did that push him toward someone easier? Why wasn't I enough? Why did he choose them? What's fundamentally wrong with me? For three years, these questions played on repeat, a playlist of self-destruction I couldn't turn off. I'd wake up at 2 AM dissecting conversations from years ago. I'd see a woman who looked like the type of girl he was drawn to, and I would spend the day comparing myself to a stranger. The obsession with "why" had become my prison.

The Body Keeps the Score

Sitting on that gallery bench, my revelation should have freed me. Instead, my heart started hammering like I'd just caught him cheating all over again. Years later, in a random art gallery, my body was reacting as if I'd just discovered the betrayal.

What I didn't understand at the time was that every time I replayed the betrayal in my head, my body couldn't tell it was a memory. Every 3 AM Google search about "signs you missed that he was cheating" sent cortisol flooding through my system. My jaw ached from grinding my teeth through imaginary conversations. My shoulders lived somewhere near my ears.

Six months into my detective phase, my doctor stared at my blood work with genuine concern. "Your inflammation markers are through the roof. Your cortisol is at dangerous levels. Are you under unusual stress?" "No," I said, confused. "That was two years ago. I'm fine now. I'm just processing life." "What does processing life look like?" He asked.

I didn't want to admit I'd spent four hours the night before analyzing his Facebook patterns from 2019, looking for clues, I'd missed. My doctor looked at me carefully. "Your body thinks you're being chased by a bear. Every day. All day." That's when it clicked. My body was keeping score of every Google search about emotional manipulation. Everything I read about surviving infidelity. Every imagined conversation where I got to say something before the line went dead. The "why" chase wasn't just emotional; it was cellular. I was programming my nervous system to stay in threat mode, teaching my body that love equals danger.

The Snake Bite Wisdom

My doctor's words about being chased by a bear reminded me of something else. The advice I'd received years earlier and completely ignored. Back when the betrayal was fresh, my mentor friend said something I'd dismissed as too simple: "When someone betrays you, obsessing over why is like being bitten by a snake, then chasing after it for an explanation while the venom spreads through your veins. She paused, while watching my confused face and said, "Heal first then ask why later or never."

I nodded politely while screaming inside. She didn't understand. How could she reduce my devastation to a nature metaphor? This wasn't some snake bite! This was my life exploding. This was being blocked mid-sentence, erased like I'd never mattered. "I hear you," I'd said, while in my mind I was planning my next Google search about emotional manipulation tactics.

She'd seen right through me. "The snake doesn't care why it bit you. And knowing why won't make the venom disappear." But standing in that gallery, watching those climbers battle through conditions that should have killed them, her words hit me with the force of an avalanche. Oh my God. She was right.

His betrayal, the cheating, the lies, the final phone call where he announced his new life and hung up; that was the snake bite. Painful and venomous but contained to that moment. My obsession with understanding it? That was the venom. Every sleepless night dissecting his psychology was venom spreading through my veins. Every hour spent decoding hidden meanings was poison working deeper into my system. I'd been literally chasing the snake for years while the poison did its work.

The antidote was never in his reasons. My mentor had tried to tell me that the antidote was in my decision to stop running. To sit down. To tend to the wound. To let the poison work its way out instead of pumping it faster through my system. I could almost hear their voice again: "The snake doesn't care why it bit you." And for the first time, I understood: Neither did he. And more importantly, neither should I.

When They Actually Give You the Why

The snake bite metaphor became even clearer when I started coaching other women through betrayal. Because here's something no one prepares you for: Sometimes the snake comes back to explain. And it changes absolutely nothing. I learned this through a client I'll call Sarah, whose story haunted me because she received everything, on her healing journey, that I thought I wanted. Sarah came to me two years into her own obsession spiral. Like me, she'd been chasing the why with the dedication of a doctoral student. She'd built entire theories about his behavior, researched attachment styles until she could diagnose strangers on the street. Her apartment looked like a detective's office with books on narcissism, printouts about emotional unavailability, and notes connecting his behaviors to his unresolved father wounds.

"If I could just understand," she told me during our first session, her eyes hollow from sleepless nights. "If I just knew why, I could finally move on." I sat there, my chest tight, because I was looking at myself. We both experienced the same desperation and conviction that understanding equals healing. Then something happened that made me grateful for my blocked number, my hung-up-on ending, and my forced silence.

He called her. Sarah's ex called two years after their breakup. He was apologetic and ready to explain everything. "I couldn't believe it," Sarah said. My hands were shaking so badly I could barely hold the phone. She'd rehearsed this moment a thousand times. Finally, she'd get her answers. He spent an hour on the phone explaining everything; his commitment issues, how his father abandoned the family when he was seven, and his deep-seated fear of intimacy. He connected every dot. His therapist had helped him see how his mother's emotional dependence made him associate love with suffocation."

I watched her face as she spoke, waiting for the relief, the peace, the closure she'd been chasing. "I kept waiting to feel it," she said, her voice breaking. "That moment everyone promises when you finally understand. The feeling of peace and closure." I didn't feel it. "What did you feel instead?" I asked, though I already knew. "Empty." The word came out like a whisper. "Hollow. Like I'd been running a marathon for two years only to discover there was no finish line."

She looked at me with tears streaming down her face. "Because every single reason he gave was about him. His wounds. His fears. His damage. His mother, his father, his childhood, his therapy breakthrough. Not one explanation, not one, had anything to do with who I was, what I deserved, or why I wasn't worth fighting his demons for." "I thought understanding his damage would undo mine," she continued. "But his clarity didn't heal anything. It just confirmed what I'd been too afraid to admit: I spent two years trying to solve a puzzle that had nothing to do with me."

That's when we both learned a hard truth: Understanding someone's reasons for hurting you doesn't undo the hurt. Their explanation is their story. Your healing is yours. And the two have nothing to do with each other.

"Do you know what the worst part is?" She asked me. I was so curious to hear her answer, I said, "Yes, tell me." She said, "I wasted two years waiting for permission to heal. Permission that could only come from him explaining why he'd hurt me. But healing was never his to give. It was always mine to take." Sarah's path became the bridge to my freedom. She got her why. And it healed nothing.

Two Women, Same Betrayal, Different Futures

After watching Sarah's empty victory, I realized the question was never the problem. The meaning I attached to the answer was. Picture two women discovering identical betrayals. Same texts. Same lies. Same gut-punch.

Woman One decides: "I'm fundamentally unlovable." She investigates obsessively, building a case file of her inadequacy. She stops eating, stops sleeping, starts therapy, but spends it dissecting his pathology instead of healing hers. She dates again but attracts the same type: emotionally unavailable men who smell her desperation. She's broadcasting the frequency of abandonment so loudly that healthy people step back while opportunists step forward.

Woman Two decides: "He showed me who he is. Now I know who I'm not settling for." Instead of investigating him, she investigates herself, not for flaws, but for patterns. She doesn't date for six months, not from fear, but from intention. She rebuilds with therapy, journaling, and cycling classes. She joins a hiking group; starts the business she'd put on hold. When she dates again, she's different: "I'm not anxious. I know what disrespect looks like now, and this isn't it." Same betrayal. Completely different futures. The formula was devastating and simple: Meaning → Emotions → Actions → Habits → Identity → Destiny

Woman One asked, "Why am I so unlovable?" and built a life that confirmed it. Woman Two asked, "What do I want now?" and built a life that created it.

I'd been Woman One for years. But I didn't have to stay her.

The Mirror Moment That Changed Everything

After realizing I could choose a different story, I found myself in my bathroom at midnight, spiraling again. Two hours deep in investigation; his social media, and our old photos. My laptop was hot from overuse, my eyes burning from screen glare, my chest tight from shallow breathing. I went to wash my face and caught my reflection. The woman in the mirror looked haunted and hollow. Like she'd been awake for weeks. Suddenly, I heard my own voice asking a question that stopped everything: "Am I spending more energy understanding why he hurt me, or protecting who I'm becoming?" The answer knocked the wind out of me.

I spent approximately 3,000 hours investigating his psyche. And I couldn't tell you what I'd done to build my own future in the last month. I knew his attachment style and his enneagram number. I lost complete sight of myself, and I no longer knew what my dreams were. That night, I closed my laptop, like shutting a coffin lid. Instead of reopening old texts for the hundredth time, I opened a fresh journal. Instead of writing "Why did he..." I wrote "She is becoming..."

The 37-Year Run

And then I met her. The woman I was becoming. I wrote about her like she already existed:

She is becoming someone who sleeps through the night. She is becoming someone who trusts her instincts. She is becoming someone who has good posture and walks with her head up. She is becoming someone who chooses peace over answers, growth over grinding, future over forensics. For the first time in three years, I planned my next moves instead of my next arguments. I chose my tomorrow over his yesterday. That night taught me the crucial difference between questions that imprison and questions that heal:

Questions that imprison:

Why wasn't I enough? Makes me the problem.

What's wrong with me? Assumes I'm broken.

Why did they choose someone else? Gives them the power.

How could they do this? Keeps me in victim mode.

Why don't they see my worth? Makes my value dependent on their vision.

Questions that heal:

What do I need right now? Centers my wellbeing.

How can I honor myself today? Makes me active, not passive.

What boundary needs to be strengthened? Focuses on my power.

What pattern am I ready to break? Points toward growth.

Who am I becoming through this? Transforms pain into purpose.

The shift was subtle but revolutionary. Imprisoning questions made him the subject and me the object. Healing questions made me the author of my own story. The quality of your questions determines the quality of your healing.

The 2 AM Protocol

Knowing and doing are different beasts, especially at 2 AM when your addiction screams loudest. That's when she's weakest, the 2 AM version of you. She's tired, vulnerable, probably a little drunk on exhaustion or wine or both. Her defenses are down. Her phone is right there. Just a quick check. Just to see. Just to know. I developed this emergency protocol for her, for when the urge to investigate feels like drowning:

Physical intervention: Put the phone in another room. Not on the nightstand. Not face down next to you. Another room. Make your body move to get to it.

Name the craving: Write down exactly what answer you're seeking. "I want to know if they're happy." "I want to see if she's prettier." "I want to know if he misses me." See it on paper. See how small it looks.

Reality check: Ask yourself, "If I had this answer, would I actually feel better?" Spoiler: You won't. You never do. You just need another hit.

Future self-intervention: Write what you'd tell your daughter or a best friend if she was doing this at 2 AM. Be the mother or parent to yourself that you'd be to her.

One healing action: Do one thing that honors your future self instead of investigating your past self. Drink water. Stretch your body. Write one paragraph describing in detail, your dreams. Pray. Text a friend "I appreciate you." Anything that builds instead of excavates.

The 2 AM version of you is the most vulnerable to the "why" addiction. She's the one who'll undo weeks of progress in a single scrolling session. Protect her fiercely. She's not weak; she's wounded. And wounds need protection while they heal.

This protocol saved me more times than I can count. Not because it made the urge go away, but because it made me pause long enough to remember, I'm not a detective anymore. I'm an architect. And architects don't build by looking backward.

Your Choice

You're standing at the same crossroads I faced in that gallery. The decision to no longer ask, "Why did they leave?" and start asking, "Who am I becoming?" This shifts everything. Your voice breaks through, clean and strong. Your body unclenches as your shoulders drop, your jaw releases, and your chest opens up. For the first time in years, you're not a detective analyzing clues in the case of your own abandonment. You're just living in the present. The moment you stop chasing people who can't see you, you become visible to people who can. This is the life that's been waiting for you; not their apology, not their return, and not in understanding their why. It's been waiting for your decision to stop being a supporting character in their story and start being the protagonist of your own.

The storm didn't defeat the climbers in that painting; it exposed their strength. Your pain doesn't have to destroy you. It can forge you into someone unshakeable. Stop chasing their why. Start protecting your who. Every moment spent understanding their brokenness is stolen from your wholeness. The person you're becoming is worth more than the explanation you're seeking. Choose yourself. Let the unanswered questions remain unanswered. What does matter is knowing that you are worth protecting, worth healing, and worth fighting for to become everything you were meant to be.

The pen is in your hand. Stop editing their story and start writing yours today.

CHAPTER THIRTEEN

How One Night Rewrote My Story

Surviving Domestic Violence and Learning to Run Toward Life

I was nineteen when I married a man who would teach me that love can be a weapon and that sometimes, survival means disappearing entirely, even from yourself. He was everything my sheltered church-girl's heart thought it wanted: feared by many, rebellious, and thrilling in all the ways my safe childhood had never been. With a criminal record and a defiant attitude, he seemed untouchable, like someone who didn't need anyone's approval. What I didn't understand then was that I was unconsciously searching for the protection I'd lost when my father died. At twelve, I learned that the man who was meant to keep me safe could vanish without warning. At nineteen, I thought I'd found someone whose strength and edge would shield me from vulnerability. I was drawn to the very darkness that should have sent me running, mistaking his capacity for violence as proof he could protect me from a world that felt dangerous. I didn't realize the person I needed protection from would be him.

The twelve-year-old girl inside me was still grieving, still longing for someone strong enough to stand between her and a world that had already proven it could take everything in a single night. I mistook his explosive temper and troubled past as signs of strength, believing they meant he could protect me. But the truth was far more painful: the very person I trusted to keep me safe became the one I needed protection from. I hadn't found shelter; I had stepped into the storm.

The 37-Year Run

Three months into the relationship, I found out I was pregnant. My value system gave me only one option: marriage. My belief system at the time said that girls who found themselves pregnant got married and built happy families. There was no room in my nineteen-year-old worldview for any other choice. I walked down the aisle loving him completely, even as a quiet voice inside me whispered that he would never love me the same way. What I didn't know was that I was trading my freedom for what I thought was security and that the next ten years would teach me survival skills I never should have needed.

Walking on Eggshells

From the beginning, our home moved to the unpredictable rhythm of his moods. I learned to read the slope of his shoulders as he walked through the door, the tone of his voice when he answered the phone, the tightness in his jaw when something had gone wrong at work. Without realizing it, I took on the role of emotional caretaker, managing the atmosphere, keeping the peace, and doing whatever I could to prevent his anger from finding a target.

I didn't leave dishes in the sink. I kept the children quiet while he watched TV. I nodded in agreement even when his opinions clashed with my own values. I became skilled at anticipating his needs and meeting them before he had to ask. It wasn't a conscious strategy; it was survival. Every woman who's lived with an angry man knows this dance. You shrink yourself little by little, hoping that if you take up less space, make less noise, and need less, maybe the storm will pass you by. But storms don't skip houses because the people inside make themselves small. They hit where they want to hit.

The Isolation Begins

His control didn't arrive all at once; it crept in quietly, disguised as concern or opinion. He didn't like my friends; they were "too churchy" or "they thought they were better than us." Over time, I stopped hanging out with them. Eventually, the only people in my life were the ones he approved of. He rarely spent time with my family, choosing instead to be at his family's house whenever he had free time. Slowly, and without realizing it, I began to let go of the people who might have seen what was really happening. The ones who loved me, who might have offered perspective or support, faded from our lives.

After our third baby in just over three years, his absences became more frequent and harder to ignore. He started spending nights at strip clubs, coming home smelling of alcohol and perfume, his clothes carrying the scent of betrayal. When I tried to talk about it, he'd explode, angry that I didn't appreciate how hard he worked, how lucky I was to have a man who provided. I learned to stop asking questions.

I poured everything I had into raising our three babies, letting motherhood become both my identity and my shield. As long as I felt like I was being a good mother, I could avoid facing the truth. I was slowly disappearing inside a marriage where I no longer existed as a wife. Toward the end of our marriage, he partnered with someone who helped him start a company. That meant long hours, unpredictable schedules, and plenty of freedom to be wherever he wanted.

The Cycle: Threat, Flee, Forgive, Repeat

The chokehold incident wasn't an isolated explosion of violence; it was the culmination of a pattern of terrorization that had been escalating for years. The calls came around 2 AM, when the bars closed, and his alcohol-fueled rage had nowhere else to go. The phone would ring, jarring me awake from whatever restless sleep I could manage, and I'd hear his voice slurred, violent, completely detached from any humanity I'd once recognized in him. "I have a gun," he'd say, his words ice-

The 37-Year Run

cold despite the drinking. "I'm coming home to kill you." The first time it happened, I thought it might be an empty threat, the kind of thing drunk people say when they're angry. But something in his tone, the flatness, the certainty, the complete lack of emotion told me he meant every word. My response became automatic; a survival protocol burned into my nervous system through repetition. I would wake up the three children, ages four, six, and seven. I helped them while they were half asleep to get into the car. I did not tell them why we were leaving the house so quickly. I did all I could to protect my kids from their dad's actions.

Then I would drive out of the neighborhood as fast as possible, hands shaking so intensely I could barely grip the steering wheel, praying we wouldn't cross paths with him on his way home. I would drive until I reached a hotel a town away because I did not want him to come looking for me. I would tell the front desk clerk, "Please don't give my room number to anyone. My husband is threatening to kill me."

I would spend the rest of the night awake, listening for footsteps outside the door, keeping my children close while they fell back asleep, confused and scared. This scenario played out too many times to count. I can't remember exactly how many 2 AM escapes we made, but I remember the bone-deep exhaustion of living in a constant state of terror, never knowing when the next one would come. Each time, the next day would bring the familiar cycle. He would call, his voice suddenly gentle, apologetic, desperate. "Valerie, I'm so sorry. I was drunk, I didn't mean it. I would never hurt you. Please come home. The kids need their dad. We're a family."

I was a young, stay-at-home mom with three young children and no fundamental understanding of domestic violence patterns. I firmly believed that love could fix broken people. I stayed because the alternative of being a single mother with no financial support felt impossibly scary. I would go back every time. Each return taught my children that danger was temporary, that adults couldn't be trusted to keep them safe, and that home was a place you might have to flee from in the middle of the night. Each return taught me that my instincts for self-preservation weren't trustworthy, that maybe I was overreacting, perhaps the problem was my inability to handle his drinking rather than his threats to kill me.

The pattern continued until the night he put his hands around my throat, and I finally understood that this wasn't about alcohol, anger management, or even marriage problems. This was about a man who was capable of killing me, and children who would be left motherless if I didn't find the courage to break the cycle permanently.

On one particular summer night, he asked me out on a date. "I have to stop by this bar first to get something from a friend," he said as we left the house. "It'll only take a few minutes." I should have known better. Nothing was ever "Just a few minutes." I sat in the car for what felt like an hour, watching people come and go from the bar, wondering if I should go in and find him or just wait.

Finally, he emerged and got into the driver's seat. The moment he closed the car door, I knew something was terribly wrong. His eyes had a look I'd never seen before, cold and distant and completely detached from the man I'd married. It was like looking at a stranger wearing my husband's face. He started the engine and began driving, but not toward any restaurant. As we drove, he started talking to me in a voice I didn't recognize, low, threatening, filled with a violence that made my blood turn cold.

I can't remember exactly what he said because my brain was too busy calculating escape routes and survival strategies. But I remember the tone, the way it made every instinct I had scream

The 37-Year Run

that I was in immediate danger. When we stopped at a red light, I saw my chance. I grabbed the door handle and tried to jump out, planning to run to the gas station on the corner and call someone to pick me up. But before I could get the door open, his arm shot across the car and grabbed me around the neck. The chokehold was immediate and terrifying.

I couldn't breathe, couldn't scream, I couldn't do anything but feel his forearm pressing against my windpipe while he spoke directly into my ear. "I'm going to break your neck and kill you," he said, his voice calm and matter-of-fact, like he was discussing the weather.

He held me like that while he drove with one arm around my neck, the other steering the car down the road. I couldn't breathe properly. Black spots danced at the edges of my vision. But somehow, I managed to whisper prayers under my breath. God, please don't let me die. Please let me see my children again. Please help me get home safely.

The Construction Site

He drove us to a remote location, his place of business. It was located down a long, dark road where no one would ever hear me scream. The lot was empty, scattered with heavy machinery. As we pulled in, he finally released the chokehold, only to replace it with a grip on my arm so tight I knew it would leave a bruise. "I'm going to dig a hole and bury you," he said, gesturing toward the excavation equipment nearby. The way he said it, calm, casual, like it was just another task, was more chilling than the threat itself. This wasn't rage. It was calculation.

He pulled me toward the excavator while I prayed silently, desperately. Please, God. Don't let this be how my children lose their mother. When he went to start the machine, the keys weren't there. He checked his pockets and the ignition, growing more agitated as he realized they were in the car. We walked back, only to find the car locked with the keys inside. He had to call someone to come and unlock it for us. That phone call saved my life. Someone now knew we were there. Someone had heard his voice and could remember the location; they could connect him to whatever might have happened.

The presence of a witness changed everything. His demeanor shifted, returning to something resembling normal as we waited for the tow truck. When the tow truck arrived and the car was unlocked, he drove me home without another word. But I knew it wasn't over. Whatever had taken hold of him that night hadn't left. It was still there, waiting for a moment without locked doors, missing keys, or inconvenient witnesses.

The Great Escape

The following week, while he was at work, I carried out an escape plan I'd been quietly preparing. I packed only the essentials, clothes for myself and the kids, important documents, and a few treasured photos. Everything else, the furniture, the dishes, and the life I'd spent seven years building, I left behind. Material things could be replaced. Our lives could not be.

I loaded my three children into the car and drove to my brother's house. I knew it wouldn't be long before we were found, but I hoped it would buy enough time to figure out what came next. What followed was a divorce that felt more like a war. He began showing up at little league games, whispering threats when he would get near me. He drove past my brother's house at odd hours, just slowly enough to be seen. Once, he jumped out from a neighbor's yard as I parked, walked up to me, and spit in my face. I called the police repeatedly. Each time, they told me the same thing: he hadn't physically harmed me yet, so there was nothing they could do. Threats weren't enough. They had to wait until he followed through. Then they could help. I lived in a constant state of hypervigilance, scanning parking lots before getting out of the car, double-checking locks, creating backup plans for even the most routine tasks.

The Rush to Feel Whole

In the midst of that terrifying chapter of my life, I met someone at a Bible study hosted by a friend. He was visiting from out of state. He appeared to be gentle, kind, and everything my former husband was not. Where one had been volatile, he was calm. Where there had been threats, he offered protection. Where there had been chaos, he promised peace. We spent hours talking on the phone. He flew in to visit a few times. Before my divorce was finalized, we had already begun planning our wedding.

I married a man I barely knew because, at the time, safety felt more important than anything else. My children had met him only a handful of times before he became their stepfather. Looking back, I can see the red flags I missed: the rushed timeline, the long-distance courtship, and the way I was making life-altering decisions from a place of trauma rather than healing.

Unprocessed pain doesn't leave room for clarity. It makes you reach for anything that promises to end the fear. Six months into that second marriage, I was pregnant with my fourth child, another baby, another chance to build the family I had always dreamed of. And, unknowingly, another way to avoid facing what I had just survived.

The Patterns That Trauma Creates

What I didn't yet understand was that surviving domestic violence had rewired my nervous system in ways that would shape every decision I made for the next twenty years. I became addicted to hypervigilance. My brain was constantly scanning for threats, interpreting everyday tension as danger, reacting to raised voices or minor disagreements as if they were signs of imminent harm. Even in safe situations, I couldn't relax. I was always on edge, easily startled, always bracing for something to go wrong.

I lost trust in my own judgment. If I had been so wrong before, mistaking control for protection, violence for passion, how could I trust myself to recognize safety or goodness in anyone else? The conflict became unbearable. Any sign of tension triggered my fight-or-flight response, and I would do anything to keep the peace, even if it meant abandoning my own needs entirely.

I became an expert in emotional weather. I could sense mood shifts in others before they were even aware of them, and I instinctively adjusted my behavior to manage their emotions. Fear became my compass. Every decision ran through one filter: Will this keep me safe? Not the question that truly mattered: is this good for me and my children? These trauma responses made perfect sense while I was in danger. The problem was, they didn't disappear when the danger did. They became my default operating system, quietly influencing every relationship, every choice, for decades.

The Price My Children Paid

The survival strategies that helped get us out alive came with a cost I wouldn't fully understand for years. In my urgency to create safety and stability, I moved my children from one father figure to another one without giving any of us time to heal. I was so focused on escaping the past that I didn't stop to consider how my choices might shape their future. They learned to be hypervigilant early, watching adults for signs of trouble,

The 37-Year Run

reading moods before words were spoken. They became experts at adjusting their behavior to match the emotional temperature of the room. Most heartbreaking of all, they learned that love meant enduring whatever treatment was given to them. They watched me accept years of emotional and physical threats in the name of keeping our family together. The lessons I hoped to teach my children about love, commitment, and family were overshadowed by the ones they actually learned like how to survive, how to accommodate, and how to navigate the dangerous terrain of adult relationships.

The Survival Skills That Became Prison Bars

The strategies that once kept me alive became the very patterns that nearly destroyed me after the danger had passed. My internal radar was so sensitive that I couldn't distinguish between real red flags and everyday friction. Everything felt like a potential threat. I lost my voice entirely. Years of learning that speaking up led to punishment made it nearly impossible for me to express my needs, set boundaries, or advocate for myself in any relationship.

I became addicted to approval. If everyone liked me, if no one was angry, maybe I could finally feel safe. I developed a compulsive need to fix and rescue others, using their problems as a distraction from my own pain. It was easier to focus outward than to face what I had survived and how deeply it had changed me. Fear became my decision-maker. I didn't ask what was right for my children or me. I went with what felt safe in the moment. These trauma-driven patterns made sense when I was in survival mode. The problem was, they didn't shut off when the danger ended. They became my default operating system, quietly shaping every romantic relationship, friendship, and parenting choice for decades.

Valerie Maksym

The Shame That Kept Me Silent

For years, I carried heavy shame, shame that shaped how I saw myself and silenced the story I was too afraid to tell. I felt ashamed for marrying someone so clearly dangerous and shame for staying as long as I did. I felt ashamed for putting my children in harm's way and for rushing into another marriage without healing. But most of all, I felt ashamed for being unable to protect my children from the consequences of my personal choices. That shame kept me silent for decades. I couldn't speak my truth because doing so would mean exposing all the ways I believed I had failed as a woman, as a mother, as someone who should have known better.

Through years of therapy, coaching, and deep healing, I've come to understand something life-changing: that shame was never mine to carry. It belonged to the circumstances, to the trauma, to the systems that failed me. And letting go of it has been one of the most powerful steps toward reclaiming my voice.

The Daughter Who Reflected Healing

Six months into my second marriage, I discovered I was pregnant with my fourth child. A baby girl. I intentionally made her initials BLS to stand for "Blessing." She has become a great blessing in my life. Brianna was born into a home that, while imperfect, was calmer than the one her older siblings had known. Watching her grow up without the constant tension that had marked her siblings' early years revealed just how deeply we'd all been affected. Her natural confidence and sense of security became a mirror, reflecting the fear that had once ruled our lives. She was living proof that something beautiful could rise from the ashes of trauma. Even when healing was messy and incomplete, she reminded me that restoration was possible. She is a blessing.

The 37-Year Run

The Healing That Had to Come

The patterns I developed during my first marriage didn't disappear when I left. They followed me into every relationship, every conflict, every moment I needed to advocate for myself or my children. It took decades of therapy, prayer, countless missteps, and the grace of those who saw past my defenses to help me face a hard truth: survival strategies have expiration dates.

The hypervigilance that once kept me alive became the anxiety that stole my peace. The people-pleasing that protected me when I was trapped turned into self-abandonment once I was free. Learning to feel safe in my own body, to trust my judgment, and to believe that conflict didn't always mean danger, this became the real work of healing.

I still remember the night I prayed in a chokehold, begging God to let me live long enough to see my children again. That prayer was answered. But the woman who survived that night was forever changed. It took me twenty years to understand: surviving is not the same as healing, and the courage required to heal is often greater than the courage it takes to survive.

Thirty-Seven Years Later: The Healing That Finally Came

This was the second-to-last chapter I wrote for this book, and I don't believe that was a coincidence. My body and mind delayed this chapter until I was finally ready to face the truth. Six days before my manuscript deadline, I sat alone in a hotel room by the beach. My husband was asleep beside me, and I stared at my laptop, knowing I had to write about the darkest part of my story.

I had already written about my father's death, my patterns of people-pleasing, and my struggle to communicate authentically. But this story, the one that explained why I developed those survival strategies in the first place, had remained locked away for decades.

As I began typing, describing the chokehold, the 2 AM escapes, the hotel rooms where I stayed awake protecting my children from a danger they couldn't yet understand; my chest tightened. My breathing grew shallow. The anxiety I thought I had processed came rushing back as if it had never left. But I kept writing. I wrote about mistaking violence for strength, about seeking protection from someone who became my greatest threat, and about the impossible choices trauma has you to make while your nervous system is stuck in survival mode.

When I finished, I walked into the bathroom, quietly closed the door, and cried, for real, bawled my eyes out. Not the polite tears shed in therapy, but the body-shaking sobs of a woman finally allowing herself to feel the full weight of what she had survived. I cried for the nineteen-year-old girl who thought she was choosing safety. For the young mother who had to make impossible decisions. For the woman who believed she deserved the pain. For all the nights I'd lie awake, listening for the sound of his car pulling in. And for all the time I made myself small, hoping to avoid his rage. I cried with relief, the kind that comes when you finally stop carrying a weight you were never meant to bear.

And when the tears subsided, something shifted. I felt lighter. I felt forgiveness for every version of myself who had done the best she could with the resources she had at the time. The girl who married her abuser. The mother who kept returning to danger. The woman who fled into another marriage without healing. They were all trying to survive. Writing this story didn't just help me process what happened, it gave me clarity I never had before.

The 37-Year Run

Healing isn't linear, and time doesn't automatically heal all wounds. Trauma can remain buried for decades, and sometimes it takes years before you feel safe enough to remember what you've survived. Some wounds need time before they're ready to be touched. Some stories need to be lived before they can be told.

I'm grateful for every piece of healing that has come, even when it arrived later than I would have liked. The woman who finally cried is now strong enough to help others see that their survival stories, however imperfect, are stories of extraordinary courage.

That night in the hotel bathroom, I wasn't just releasing fear. I was honoring the woman who kept me and my children alive when staying alive felt impossible. She deserved those tears. She deserved compassion. And so do you, if you see yourself on these pages. You are not broken, weak, or less intelligent. You are a survivor who developed exactly the skills you needed to stay alive in impossible circumstances. Those skills may no longer serve you, but they were brilliant adaptations to the reality you faced. Healing means honoring the person who saved your life, even as you learn new ways to live it.

The scared girl, the desperate mother, and the traumatized woman I once was, she did what she had to do to survive. Now, it's time to help her thrive. That night in the chokehold, when my vision blurred at the edges and my lungs screamed for air, I prayed to live long enough to see my children again. I am forever thankful that my prayers were answered that night. Today, I sit back and observe as each one of my children builds healthy relationships, sets boundaries, and makes decisions from courage instead of fear. My children didn't inherit all of my trauma. I broke the cycle, the one that could have infected generations, when I chose healing over hiding.

Valerie Maksym

That prayer in the darkness wasn't just answered; it was transformed into something beautiful. Something whole. Something that proves survival is only the beginning. The real victory doesn't come from enduring the pain; it comes when you stop surviving and start living. When you stop running and start healing. When you realize that life doesn't reward those who merely endure, it rewards those who dare to transform. And the moment you decide to rise, you don't just rewrite your own story. You become living proof that change has no expiration date, that healing is possible, that the runway you've been circling for years is finally clear for takeoff.

CHAPTER FOURTEEN

The Pilot I Finally Named

The Day I Switched Seats with God

The afternoon I heard that Charlie Kirk had died, I was typing mid-sentence when my fingers froze above the keyboard. I closed my laptop and went still, as if stillness could somehow undo the news. The apartment was quiet, but inside me, a thousand thoughts collided; shock, anger, confusion, disbelief, all of them fighting for space in my chest. Then, cutting through the chaos like a blade of clarity, a single steady sentence rose up: You were never meant to fly through this life alone.

The Weight of Silent Faith

As long as I can remember, I've always been a believer. I was raised in the church since birth. I prayed in parking lots before meetings, windows up so no one would see my lips moving. I kept my Bible tucked away on a bookshelf. When people asked what got me through my darkest moments, I'd credit my "inner strength," or I'd tell a story about how I figured out the solutions to what I was going through. I told myself I wanted to be respectful of others' beliefs, because not everyone is a Christian. However, sitting there with the news of Charlie's death heavy in my chest, I finally admitted the truth: I was a coward. Not the kind of coward who runs from physical danger, but the kind who runs from the judgement of others. The kind who'd rather suffocate slowly than risk the discomfort of someone rolling their eyes at my faith. The kind who'd edit

The 37-Year Run

God out of my own testimony because I didn't want to be "that person," who sounded all religious.

In that moment of silence, I bowed my head for Charlie and felt something shift inside me, something fundamental and irreversible. The truth I'd been running from for thirty-seven years finally caught up with me. I had spent years telling a story about my airplane, about the baggage, the runway, and the lift. But I hadn't told the truth that mattered most: I'd been muscling the controls by myself. For a long time, my faith was part of the baggage I carried, but I never unpacked it in front of others. I prayed. I listened. I felt God guiding me in the quiet, but I rarely said His name out loud. Fear kept my faith small. Fear of getting into an argument or debate, I didn't have the energy to fight. Fear of judgment from people whose approval I thought I needed. Fear that speaking His name would cost me opportunities, relationships, and relevance. So, I played it safe and kept it private, called it "being respectful" when what I really meant was "being afraid."

The Cost of Hidden Faith

You want to know what hiding your faith costs? Everything. It cost me authenticity; and being authentic is one of my top core beliefs. I became an expert at telling 99% of my story, while leaving out the crucial 1% that explained how I survived. It cost me connection; I attracted people who loved my edited version, not my whole truth. It cost me power; every miracle I'd experienced got rewritten as coincidence; every divine intervention became "lucky timing." But most of all, it cost me peace. Because when you're constantly monitoring yourself, constantly filtering, constantly afraid someone will discover what actually sustains you, you're never really free. You're performing even in your most vulnerable moments.

Valerie Maksym

The Charlie I Knew

I was new to watching the college campus debates with Charlie Kirk. I'd watched him stand and debate in spaces where his faith made him a target. I watched him take the hits, the mockery, the dismissals, and yet he remained firm in his beliefs. Not with anger, but with this quiet certainty that what he believed was worth the cost of believing it out loud.

He didn't weaponize his faith or use it to divide. He simply refused to hide it. He refused to pretend that God wasn't the center of his story. And in a world that increasingly demands we keep our faith in carefully controlled private spaces, his refusal was revolutionary. What struck me most wasn't his boldness; it was his peace. You can't fake that kind of peace. You can't manufacture it through positive thinking or meditation apps. That peace only comes from knowing who's really flying the plane.

Watching Charlie stand firmly grounded in what he believed, agree with him or not, did something in me. It reminded me that conviction doesn't scream; it stands. His boldness nudged me to be honest about mine. If I'm going to write a book about letting go, I have to tell you the whole story of what and who held me together while I was laying things down.

From Pilot to Co-Pilot

Here's my revelation: I am no longer the pilot of my plane. I am capable, yes, trained by pain, strengthened by practice, but I'm not the one charting the wind or controlling the weather. I've tried to white-knuckle the yoke through storms I didn't cause and turbulence I couldn't calm down. On the evening of Sept. 10, I made a decision to slide out of the pilot's seat. I put God where He belonged all along, in control. I took the co-pilot's seat, hands ready, heart open, and eyes on the instruments of grace. That's not a slogan; it changed the way I live. My prayer

The 37-Year Run

time isn't an afterthought anymore; it's a pre-flight ritual. Scripture isn't theory; it's my checklist. Community isn't optional; it's my ground crew. And the Holy Spirit? My guidance system, quietly correcting course, whispering when to climb, when to wait, and when to land.

Naming the Root: Fear of Judgment

I didn't see it until now: so much of my life I lived in a state of paralysis because I was terrified of judgment. I wasn't just afraid of failing; I was fearful of being told I was wrong. That same fear also slipped quietly into my spiritual life. I kept my faith tucked away, careful not to offend or be corrected. That caution cost me courage.

Here's the truth I'm ready to say out loud. I haven't given God the credit He deserves. It is only because of Him that I'm standing. Only because of Him that the traumas of my past no longer run my present. Only because of Him that unforgiveness isn't taking up space in my heart. I have forgiven those who hurt me, and I pray that anyone I've hurt over the years could forgive me, too. That's not my strength, that's His grace.

I've been told that you can really understand life by looking back and connecting the dots of the highs and the lows; it all tells a story. When I trace back on my healing journey, I see the "aha" moments weren't accidents. The vision on the side of the road is clear. The courage to forgive. The strength to set boundaries. The peace that made no sense. Those dots form a line I didn't draw by myself. God was there, steady in every chapter, lifting, correcting, healing, and giving me eyes to see what I could finally release.

I once believed I figured life out. From the framework, the formulas, and the methods I have learned over the years; I now know they were gifts. He handed me the following piece to my puzzle of life; only when my hands were free to hold it. He healed me by opening my eyes, giving me insight piece by piece, until I could carry the truth without collapsing under it. I can't edit Him out of my own miracle. Father God, I release the fear of judgment; be my pilot today and give me courage to live my faith openly.

A Poem From Me to Charlie: The Man Who Stood

You stood when standing cost you, In rooms where faith was mocked, Not with fists or fury rising, But with truth that can't be blocked.

You didn't hide behind comfort, Didn't whisper what you knew, While I sat silent in my shadows, Too afraid to stand with you.

Your death became my wake-up call, A bell I can't unhear, That life half-lived in hidden faith Is life controlled by fear.

You showed me courage isn't loud, It's standing in your truth, It's refusing to apologize For the God who carried you through.

I never knew you personally, but you changed my life's whole arc, You taught me that a hidden light can't pierce anyone's dark.

So now I stand where you once stood, though my knees may shake with fear, I'll speak the name I've hidden long: Jesus Christ, my pilot here.

Thank you for the confrontation Your life became to mine, for showing me that faith concealed is leaving God behind.

Rest now, warrior, your battle's done, your testimony stays: That those who stand for what they love Light others' darkest days.

I promise this, though we never met, your courage lit my way, I'll stand in truth, I'll speak His name, Beginning from today.

The 37-Year Run

A Letter I Felt Compelled to Write

Charlie, thank you for standing in your truth. Your courage pushed me out of hiding. Your life, and your death, woke something in me I was afraid to name. Because you stood in your truth, it's given me the courage to stand in mine. Rest, and I will do my best to stand in my truth and be courageous in the process.

Lord, thank you for never leaving the cockpit when I was terrified, when I was stubborn, and when I was silent about your goodness. You wrote this book long before I typed a word. You were the constant thread; the quiet strength woven through every chapter, lifting each page.

What This Means

I'm not flying solo anymore. I invite God into the daily decisions I make, not just the damage. I lead with honesty, not hidden agendas. My faith isn't a footnote; it's the headline. I let God set the weight limit. If it costs me my peace or exceeds the weight limit, it won't be allowed on the plane.

A Simple Practice: Hands Off the Yoke

Pre-flight prayer: "God, you are the pilot of my life. Lead me." Checklist of truth: One verse, one promise, one boundary for the day. Mid-air check: When anxiety spikes, say out loud: "I'm not flying this alone." Breathe and adjust course. Log the landing: At night, write one sentence: Where did God meet you in the turbulence today?

To Those Still Hiding

If you are a Christian and you're reading this with your faith tucked safely in your pocket, I see you. I was you. Maybe you're afraid of being labeled narrow-minded. Maybe you're worried about what others will think. Maybe you've convinced yourself that private faith is enough. But here's what I know now: God didn't save you to be a secret. He didn't heal you so you could pretend you healed yourself. He didn't carry you through hell, so you could give credit to "the universe." You don't have to preach on street corners. You don't have to debate or defend or fight. You just have to stop hiding. Stop editing Him out of your story. Stop pretending that your strength comes from anywhere other than where it actually comes from.

Charlie's death taught me that life is too short and too precious to live it in disguise. We get one chance to be who we authentically are, to stand for all that we believe and to give credit where credit is desperately due. Your faith isn't meant to be hidden. It's meant to be lived. Out loud. In full color. With your whole chest. The world needs to see people who've been broken and rebuilt by grace. They need to know that there's a pilot who can fly through any storm. They need to witness what it looks like when someone stops trying to fly alone. This is my declaration: I will no longer hide my faith to make others comfortable. I will no longer minimize God to maximize my acceptability. I will no longer pretend that I'm flying this plane by myself. God is my pilot. Jesus Christ is my savior. The Holy Spirit is my guide. And I'm finally brave enough to say it with the lights on.

Dedication

This chapter is my heartfelt thank-you to Charlie for the nudge that helped me stand, and to my Lord and Savior, Jesus Christ, for being the pilot of my life. I once believed my airplane couldn't fly because of the weight of the bags I carried around daily. That was partly true. The hard truth is this: a plane without a pilot never leaves the ground. It's just potential. On the day I chose my pilot, everything shifted; the horizon opened.

The 37-Year Run

If you're reading this with your hands aching from gripping the controls, here's your invitation: slide into the right seat. Say the quiet truth out loud. Let God do what you've been trying to do in your own strength. Close your eyes, unclench your jaw, and whisper, "You fly. I'll trust you." Then watch the same sky you once feared become the place you finally begin to soar through, reaching new places and heights you never thought possible.

I will close with this verse: John 3:16 (NIV): "For God so loved the world that he gave his one and only Son, that whoever believes in him shall not perish but have eternal life."

Epilogue
The Wonder Woman Discovery

Have you ever wondered how you can master one area of life while failing spectacularly in another? I was watching Tony Robbins coach a successful man when the truth hit me like a splash of cold water. He was explaining how we can be successful in one area of our life and unsuccessful in other areas. Like the CEO who commands boardrooms but struggles in his intimate relationships. The devoted parent who raises incredible, healthy children while their own body breaks down. The elite athlete who conquers every physical challenge but drowns in emotional chaos. That's when I saw it, my own fractured reflection staring back at me.

For years, people saw me as an embodiment of strength and discipline. On the bodybuilding stage, I was unstoppable. I showed up at 4:30 AM for cardio, whether I felt like it or not. Weeks before a competition, I'd spend two hours a day on the stair stepper, one in the morning, one at night. No excuses. No negotiations. I followed my nutrition plan to the gram, tracked every macro, and never missed a workout. In that arena, I felt like Wonder Woman.

I had cultivated unshakable confidence, relentless persistence, and the mental toughness to push through when my body wanted to quit. What I did or didn't do during prep showed up on stage. No one could do the work for me. I was dialed in, disciplined, and prepared for success.

But when it came to building my speaking and coaching business, my true passion, I showed up as my broken, unhealed twelve-year-old self. The same woman who could leg press four times her body weight would run from difficult conversations. The competitor who never missed a workout would skip networking events when they felt intimidating. The athlete who thrived under pressure would procrastinate on launching programs, fearing, "What if I fail?" In health and fitness, I showed up as my healthy, empowered self. In business and relationships, I showed up as my twelve-year-old self who learned that when things get hard, you sweep it under the rug and run from the pain.

Here's what I finally understood: healing isn't compartmentalized, but our coping mechanisms are. I had developed incredible discipline and resilience in the gym because it felt safe. The feedback was immediate. The rules were clear. Success was measurable. But I hadn't applied those same skills to the areas where my deepest wounds lived.

The breakthrough came when I realized I needed to bring my wonder woman mindset to my most vulnerable places. The same consistency that built my physique could build my confidence. The same discipline that got me stage-ready could heal my relationship patterns. The same refusal to quit that earned me trophies could transform my business fears.

Now I understand why so many high achievers struggle to succeed across the board. We excel in areas of our life where the pain of staying the same is greater than the pain of change. We master skills in our "safe zones" while leaving our wounded areas untouched, wondering why success in one area doesn't automatically heal the others. True transformation requires showing up as your most powerful self in every area of your life, especially the ones that scare you most.

Final Words to the Reader

You've made it to the end of this book, but this isn't an ending; it's a runway. For thirty-seven years, I ran. From pain, from truth, from the person I was meant to become. My plane sat on the tarmac, engines running, burning fuel, going nowhere. Maybe yours has been doing the same. But here's what I know now, and what I need you to know: You don't have to wait for the fear to leave before you take off. You don't need perfect conditions to fly. You just need to release the brakes. That's it. That's the secret. Your engines are already running. Your wings are already strong enough. The runway has always been clear. You've just been sitting there with the brakes locked, throttle at idle, waiting for some magical moment when taking off would feel safe. It never will.

So here's what you do: Release the brakes. Pull that throttle back fully. Give it everything you've got. Don't inch forward; LAUNCH. Don't look back at the ground you're leaving. Don't second-guess whether you have enough speed. Don't calculate if you're ready. Just go for it. Full throttle. No hesitation. No half-measures. When you commit to takeoff, you commit completely. There's no such thing as a cautious takeoff; you either give it everything or you stay grounded forever.

My Final Challenge

Choose one area of your life where you've been idling on the runway. You know the one where you've been playing small, holding back, waiting for "someday." Maybe it's the book you haven't written. The conversation you haven't had. The dream you haven't chased. The faith you haven't declared. The love you haven't risked. Show up there, full throttle. Show up with the same fierce determination that got you through your worst days. Bring the strength that helped you survive what should have destroyed you. Bring the wisdom your wounds have taught you. Bring the courage your healing has built.

Don't wait to feel ready, ready is a lie fear tells. Don't wait to feel fearless; courage only exists in the presence of fear. Don't wait for permission; you've already earned it by surviving. Start scared. Start messy. Start with your hands shaking and your voice cracking. But start. Today. Now. With your next breath. Pull back that throttle and don't let go until you're airborne.

The Truth I Leave You With

The world doesn't need a perfect version of you. Perfect is a costume that keeps you hidden. The world needs the real you; scarred, healing, rising. The you who knows that broken can be beautiful. The you who understands that transformation isn't a destination you arrive at, but a decision you make over and over, moment by moment, choice by brave choice.

You are not behind; you're exactly where you need to be. You are not broken; you're breaking open to become. You are not too late; you're right on time for your own life.

Every page you've read, every tear you've shed, every truth you've faced has been preparing you for this moment. The moment you stop asking "why me?" and start saying "watch me." The moment you switch from passenger to pilot. The moment you stop running and start rising.

Your Life Is Waiting

Make the bold decision to live the life your healing has made possible. The life where you stop carrying what isn't yours. Where you stop apologizing for taking up space. Where you stop editing your faith out of your story. Where you stop chasing why and start protecting who.

Your plane has been cleared for takeoff. The runway is yours. The sky has been waiting for you all along. And if you ever forget how strong you really are, if the old triggers return, if fear tries to ground you again, if you find yourself back on the runway afraid to fly, come back to these pages. They'll remind you that someone else sat where you're sitting, felt what you're feeling, feared what you're fearing, and still found a way to fly.

I believe in you. Not because you're perfect, but because you're still here. Still reading. Still fighting. Still choosing to heal. That's all the proof I need that you're ready. Now release those brakes. Pull back that throttle. Give it everything you have. Don't look down. Don't look back. Look forward to the horizon that's been calling your name. Go for it. Full power. No apologies. No hesitation.

P.S. - Remember: You were never meant to fly through this life alone. Let go of the controls. Trust your Pilot. And watch how high you can soar when you stop trying to fly solo. The view from up here? It's worth every moment of terror it took to leave the ground.

See you in the sky. — *Valerie*

www.ingramcontent.com/pod-product-compliance
Lightning Source LLC
Chambersburg PA
CBHW062217080426
42734CB00010B/1919